# Planning for Educatio

Also available from Continuum

*Teaching Teachers* – Angi Malderez and Martin Wedell
*How to Design a Training Course* – Peter Taylor

# Planning for Educational Change

---

## Putting people and their contexts first

**Martin Wedell**

continuum

**Continuum International Publishing Group**
The Tower Building                                     80 Maiden Lane, Suite 704
11 York Road                                           New York, NY 10038
London, SE1 7NX

www.continuumbooks.com

**British Library Cataloging-in-Publication Data**
A catalogue record for this book is available from the British Library.

ISBN: 9780826487278 (paperback)

**Library of Congress Cataloging-in-Publication Data**
A catalog record for this book is available from the Library of Congress.


Typeset by YHT Ltd, London
Printed and bound in Great Britain by MPG Books, Cornwall

# Contents

To colleagues in education worldwide, who are doing their best to ensure that (poorly planned) national educational change initiatives do benefit their learners.

# Introduction

## Terminology: Change innovation or reform?

Writers use a number of terms to talk about change in education. Formal changes at national, regional or institutional levels whose implementation has apparently been fully thought through and planned may be referred to in the literature as educational *innovations*. Sometimes large-scale national changes to, for example, the content, structure or hoped-for outcomes of a national curriculum, or to methods or formats of high-stakes assessment are referred to as educational *reforms*. I believe that very similar issues influence the outcomes of educational *innovations*, *reforms* or *changes*. In this book I therefore use the single word 'change' to refer to all alterations or adjustments to the process or content of education, whoever initiates them, and whatever their scale or degree of prior planning.

## General introduction

Educational changes can come in many forms. They may be intended to affect a single institution or a whole country. The desired goals of the change may be simple (such as changing the daily timetable in a single school) or very complex (for example, introducing a new national curriculum that implies very different approaches to teaching and learning in all schools). Whatever its scale or level of complexity, a planned educational change will more or less directly involve different groups of people. Those involved may view the prospect of change differently according to, for example, their:

- happiness with the existing state of affairs
- level of interest in professional development
- experiences of previous changes
- familiarity/sympathy with the ideas underpinning any proposed change
- confidence in their local and national leadership
- satisfaction with their existing salaries/working conditions

Even within a single country people live and work in a range of geographical, socio-economic and institutional contexts. These contexts too may differ in how supportive they can be of an educational change, for example in the extent to which:

- material conditions in most educational institutions in a country or region are supportive of the ideas that the change intends to introduce
- their local or institutional organisational culture is one that is likely to be supportive of the change process
- they have human resources (for example institutional leaders and teacher trainers) with the capacity to adequately support the change implementation process

Given the above variations and constraints, it seems obvious to me that planning for and implementing educational change is bound to be complicated, and that the visible outcomes of change are unlikely to be identical and/or to become apparent at the same speed in all institutions or classrooms. However, there is still a tendency for national educational change policy makers and planners in different parts of the world to ignore the *human* factors that strongly influence change processes. Instead they view the change process as a purely linear, rational-technical planning and legislative matter. Such an approach seems to assume that once the policy decision to initiate change has been taken, any necessary legislation passed and funding secured, successful change implementation is merely a matter of issuing clear instructions to those lower down the administrative hierarchy to introduce changes in the classroom from a given date. This approach does not seem a very likely recipe for success to me, and indeed, in terms of fully achieving their stated educational aims, many educational change initiatives are not very successful.

The idea that *people* – what they believe and how they behave – have a critical influence on the outcomes of educational (or indeed any) change initiatives is not at all new. What I wish to address in this book is the need to develop a simple, comprehensible, widely applicable approach to planning that does acknowledge *people's* central role in determining the rate and route of a change process. Section 3 of this book offers such an approach.

## Who this book is for

First, this book will be of value to educational-change practitioners worldwide who are responsible at any level for the planning and/or implementation and/or monitoring of changes within an institution, a locality or a region. These might include:

- regional, provincial, city or district level educational planners and administrators tasked with leading the implementation of national educational-change policy in their area

- leaders/heads of department in educational institutions at all levels who are responsible for planning and monitoring the implementation of change in their institutional/departmental environment
- classroom teachers interested in finding out how a change process in which they are participating might be better managed and supported, and how they could help themselves to cope with it better
- trainers/teacher educators who are responsible for planning, designing and teaching courses intended to introduce classroom teachers and/or educational administrators to the rationale for, and implications for practice of, a national educational change
- staff in government departments or NGOs worldwide who are responsible for making decisions about funding and/or planning and/or implementing educational aid initiatives, or for training staff who (are going to) lead/work on such initiatives

A second group for whom the book will be useful (and who may well include representatives of some of the above) are those teaching or studying on formal or informal courses in which discussion/analysis or practical investigation of some or all aspects of leading and/or planning and/or implementing educational change is a component. Members of this group might include:

- masters level or accredited short course students on Educational (Project) Management, Educational Leadership, Curriculum Planning and Design, Assessment and Evaluation, Teacher Education and TESOL programmes
- tutors/trainers on informal training programmes whose brief is to develop understanding of the main issues that it is wise to consider when planning or trying to implement any educational change process, the relationships between them and what can be done to support all those involved
- tutors and students on initial teacher education programmes, which hope to prepare trainees to cope and grow professionally in what is likely to be a very changeable century

## Who am I?

I would like to say a little about myself for two main reasons. One is that many people now understand the reading–writing process as a form of interaction or dialogue, and it is difficult (probably impossible) to feel involved in any dialogue if one has no idea whom one is 'talking/listening to'. Second, given that many of the large-scale educational change initiatives in the world that I refer to tend to focus on changing aspects of national *school* systems, you might wonder what I, currently working in a British university, know about the real issues that those responsible for leading or implementing educational change processes in schools worldwide have to face. I share some of your scepticism about over-reliance on 'experts' to guide educational change initiatives (see chapter 2.1), but I hope that sharing my professional background with you will help you to understand why I feel that I have something to say.

I spent over twenty years living and working in education systems in Africa, the Middle East, the Far East and Central Europe, often in contexts where national state education systems were undergoing greater or lesser changes to the content, process and expected outcomes of their school English teaching provision. The role and desired outcomes of the study of English in schools has undergone profound changes in most parts of the world over the past two or three decades, as policy makers have begun to view 'knowledge' of English as an ever more central feature of general education for learners who wish to succeed in a globalising world. My work involved planning for and/or implementing changes to curricula, materials, the content and format of assessment and teacher education provision.

This experience provided me with several clear examples of the close links that exist between education and politics. I have seen how urgent demands for changes to the content and process of education may emerge from ideological changes in national or global political and economic environments. I have seen the negative effects of such urgency on the quality of change planning at first hand, and also the effects of poor planning on the different groups of people that any educational change affects. I have met and worked with teachers, institutional leaders and local educational administrators who have been 'required' to participate in the implementation of more or (often) less well-planned top-down changes. One impetus to write this book was strongly prompted by what I know of the – often needlessly unhappy – experiences of those I met.

Since returning to the UK I have worked almost exclusively with early to mid-career education professionals from all over the world. Ongoing discussions with them suggest that the introduction of larger- and smaller-scale educational change initiatives continues to be widespread. They also suggest that approaches to the planning and implementation of such initiatives have changed surprisingly little over the past twenty years and that evidence of truly successful change is still rare.

## Why I have written this book

In my experience it is truly rare to encounter an educational-change context in which most of those involved at different levels share a common understanding of the 'why', 'what' and 'how' of change, and so are able to work collaboratively to try to achieve change aims. I have met educational administrators and/or institutional leaders whose sole introduction to a national educational change that they are supposed to 'lead' in their area has been a document from 'above', containing so little detailed information about how the change might be implemented that they are uncertain about how to proceed. More frequently I have met classroom teachers trying (usually) to do their best to implement change in their classrooms, even when they do not fully understand the reasons for/aims of the change and/or are working in conditions that positively hinder their implementation efforts. A first reason for writing this book is therefore to try to contribute to a process of making educational change a less painful process for those involved.

If an educational-change project is not perceived as achieving its intended outcomes, in terms of learner behaviour or ultimate performance, it tends to be the teachers who are the first to be blamed or otherwise made to feel as if they are primarily responsible. A further reason for writing is to try and demonstrate that teachers are only *one* of several groups of people inside and outside an education system whose participation affects the outcome of an educational-change initiative. While it is teachers who will ultimately determine whether most learners benefit from the changes, I think it is important to understand that teachers can only be expected to play their central role in the process if other groups have played, and are playing, theirs.

My third reason is that I think further discussion of educational change and how it can be made to 'work' better is extremely timely. My experience suggests that much of the teaching and learning visible in (especially school-level) classrooms worldwide continues to reflect various versions of a long-standing view that education should principally be concerned with the efficient transmission of a body of fairly stable knowledge from expert/teacher to learner. Meanwhile the tone of much recent educational rhetoric suggests that that alternatives are being sought, as education systems worldwide increasingly recognize that 'education' conceived of as above does not adequately prepare citizens for today's changing world. The twenty-first century is therefore likely to be a period of great change in education systems internationally, as national policy makers try to understand and develop alternative means of providing their citizens with an education that will help them acquire the skills and understandings needed for the continuing, and also rapidly changing, challenges of techno-globalization.

In most countries education budgets and the availability of qualified personnel of all kinds are limited. National educational-change initiatives are very expensive in both financial and human terms. The literature suggests that a virtually infinite set of interdependent variables may affect the extent to which, and speed with which, a recognizable version of an educational change becomes visibly implemented in (the majority of) classrooms, or indeed whether there is any change at all. I believe that a limited number of more universal human and material variables lie at the core of this infinite set. My final reason for writing is therefore to propose an approach that I believe can help educational leaders, especially local leaders, to carry out a quick 'baseline study' of these limited but important variables in their own area. The information that even a hasty or partial study provides is likely (if able to be acted on) to help make implementation planning more contextually appropriate. This, I believe, will in turn make it more likely that a degree of 'real' (albeit locally adjusted) change implementation can begin in most classrooms in their area, so justifying the national investment in change.

## What is in the book

It is difficult to know where to begin when considering a topic as complex as educational change. After all, changes may be introduced in widely different cultural contexts and may vary enormously in their scope. Some may aim to affect every subject in every school, others only some aspect of a single subject or single institution. The discussion and examples in this book deal mostly with the planning and implementation of national-level changes to aspects of teaching and learning a single subject (English) at primary- or secondary-school level. However, I believe (and try to show in chapters 8–10) that there are questions that can be asked whose answers can usefully inform the planning/implementation of change whatever its scale, and whatever the subject or level, within any education system.

To try to make sense of the topic area, I have chosen to divide the book into three sections. In the first section I survey some ideas from the educational-change literature (most of which comes from the English-speaking world). I use this, filtered through my own experience of being involved in change processes, to note what seems to have been learned so far about the nature of educational change, especially in terms of the issues that it seems most important to consider at the planning and implementation stages. Most educational change involves a degree of 'reculturing'. Every real educational change also takes place in a context. In order to understand what reculturing will mean for people in any particular context, it is necessary to understand people's existing 'cultures'. I therefore briefly explore the idea of educational and organizational cultures. It is these cultures, I suggest, that influence both how national policy makers approach the decision to initiate and plan a change, and how they, their representatives at local level, institutional leaders and teachers approach the detailed work of change implementation.

In the second section of this book, I consider three case studies of educational-change projects that I have more or less directly participated in. For each case, I introduce the context and the apparent rationale underlying the change. I then analyse aspects of the change initiation and implementation in the light of issues from the discussion in section 1. I particularly try to show how lack of care and thoughtfulness at change initiation and implementation stages can impact on the feelings and behaviours of the people who are most closely affected, as well as of course on the ultimate achievement of change aims.

In section 1, I try to highlight some central issues, and in section 2 some effects of their absence or presence are considered. In section 3 I suggest a small number of questions that I believe planners/policy makers in any context could usefully ask (formally or informally) to help identify how these issues are likely to affect the route and rate of change implementation in *their* context. I believe that even fairly limited answers to these questions can (if the answers are broadly honest) provide a bank of contextually relevant information to help inform the initial change conceptualizing and/or implementation planning stages. I demonstrate what I mean by asking and answering these questions for three example educational-change scenarios, and discuss what the answers can tell planners about their change context in terms of, for example:

- who and/or what the change is most likely to affect
- what the effects are likely to be
- what decisions and/or plans they need to make to support the change-implementation process
- in what order these decisions/plans could most sensibly be taken to ensure that they build on, and so support, each other as fully as possible

Each section is followed by a list of references, and sections 1 and 2 by some suggestions for further reading.

## Ways of using this book

I know that in educational change environments decisions often need to be made quickly and that on courses there is always too much to read. I therefore make a few suggestions below for readers whose time is limited.

**If you are involved in planning for/implementing an educational change process at any level,** you might feel from looking at the Contents list that it would be sensible to go straight to section 3 of the book to see what questions I suggest and perhaps whether my 'answers' make sense in your context. This would definitely be a possible starting point. However, if you are to use any of the information that you find as a result of asking your own questions, as section 3 suggests (especially if using this information involves persuading others to do things differently), you will probably be more persuasive if you have already looked at section 1 of the book.

When introducing people to new ideas it is always helpful to have some idea of their starting points. **If you are planning or designing programmes or documents to support other people's understandings of the background to an educational change and/or what it implies for practice,** you might begin by looking at chapter 3 in section 1 of the book, and considering how the main features of your cultural context are likely to influence the ideas, expectations and concerns of the people you will be working with. You might then want to skim the cases in section 2 to see if these are at all similar to your own situation and then use what you know about your context to try and answer the questions in section 3 for your context. These answers will hopefully (depending on how much time you have) enable you to design your sessions/documents to maximise the support they offer.

Almost anyone who has worked, or indeed studied, within an education system for more than a few years will have experienced some level of educational change. **If you are teaching/studying a programme that includes a focus on one or more aspects of the educational change process,** I suggest that before reading you think about your own positive or negative experiences of change, and then, while reading, consider the extent to which any of the factors identified as important in the book can help explain them.

Although novice teachers may not be conscious of any changes that affected the education system while they were at school, it is certain that they will experience change during their professional lives as teachers. **If you are teaching on an initial teacher education programme** it is appropriate to acknowledge this point. The first section of this book might usefully raise trainees' awareness of some of the issues they are likely to encounter during their professional careers. The second section might help them understand some of the factors within and outside education that can influence how people actually experience the change process.

Section 1:

# Understanding Educational Change

# Setting the scene

I have worked in state-system educational settings in different parts of the world for over twenty years. Each such system has been subject to frequent policy changes affecting, for example, areas such as school curricula (and hoped-for curriculum outcomes) and/or teaching materials and/or modes of assessments and/or recommended teaching approaches. The manner in which educational changes have been introduced in the local areas or institutions in which I worked, has in most cases been through documents sent from, or meetings arranged by, a national ministry of education. These to differing degrees outlined a rationale for the changes, the hoped-for outcome of the changes and set a deadline for their implementation.

Documents were often phrased in terms of what the proposed change 'required' or 'expected' of teachers, and I expect that you would agree that ultimately it is what teachers and learners do in a classroom that determines what an educational change will achieve in any setting. However, my experience strongly suggests that, if educational changes are to stand much chance of affecting what happens in the classroom, it is usually not only teachers who have to change. Local-level educational administrators, teacher educators, school leaders, test designers, learners and often even the wider public may all, to differing degrees, be affected by large-scale educational-change processes. Policy makers' lack of consideration of the wider change environment extending *beyond* the classroom when planning hoped-for changes *in* the classroom is, I believe, one important reason why so many large-scale educational-change initiatives may fail to achieve their aims.

The focus of this book is on supporting the local or institutional planning and/or implementation of educational change. However, since local-level changes are usually the result of policy decisions made at regional or national levels, I begin by proposing two possible national-level educational-change scenarios. They represent tendencies that I have encountered in a number of different contexts. I introduce them here because they in turn introduce some of the questions and themes that are central to this book and which will be returned to time and again throughout it. In that sense they 'set the scene' for what is to come.

Situation 1
*After a change of government, a decision is made to decentralize the national school system. Previously all educational institutions and classroom teachers had to strictly follow syllabuses and materials provided by the central government's Ministry of Education. The emphasis was on achieving a high degree of uniformity in what was taught to learners nationwide, and in how it was taught. Learners worked through the same textbooks at more or less the same speed before taking centrally administered national examinations based on these syllabuses.*

*The new government plans to change the balance of the educational decision-making process. Instead of the very strictly specified curriculum and syllabus guidelines that were previously the norm, it provides only a broad curriculum framework for the various levels of education. It retains control of national examinations, but devolves decision making on how curriculum time is divided up, exact subject content, choice of materials and teaching approaches to local educational administrators, institutional leaders and teachers. They are officially encouraged to make these decisions bearing the needs of their particular context, and especially their learners, in mind.*

Situation 2
*Teachers at all levels of the school system are used to having a great deal of autonomy about how they approach the teaching of content for all subjects. There are syllabuses for each subject and all pupils take the same national exam. Of course, teachers and learners wish to do well in these, but it is acknowledged that exams cannot assess everything that it hoped will be learnt. Teachers are free to make many of their own choices about the extent to which they focus on particular aspects of the syllabus content, and about what material and teaching approaches they choose to use to provide an all-round education and to prepare learners for the exams.*

*A new government decides that the existing situation results in too much variation in the quality of teaching and learning in different classrooms and institutions. A more detailed formal written national curriculum is required. This is duly introduced. It provides extremely detailed guidelines as to both subject content and its timing, and to the pedagogical principles that teachers should follow. All teachers are expected to teach according to these guidelines. Exam league tables are published annually to show the general public how successful the learners in each school have been in standardized national exams based on the new curriculum.*

---

QUESTIONS TO CONSIDER
Which of the above situations is closer to the situation in your own educational context?
How would you feel if you were suddenly expected to shift from your current situation to the other one?
Who else, apart from teachers, would be directly affected by any such shift?

---

In my experience, an immediate reaction to an abrupt unsupported shift from one situation to the other among those who will be affected (local administrators, institutional leaders, inspectors as well as teachers) is likely to be some form of visible or invisible 'resistance'. In situation 1 a reason for such 'resistance' may be people's lack of confidence in their ability to fulfil all the unaccustomed roles that they have suddenly been made responsible for. In situation 2 'resistance' may result from a feeling of anger at the implicit suggestion that the national authorities no longer regard those working in education as sufficiently professional to be trusted to continue to make their own decisions.

| Situation 1 | Situation 2 |
| --- | --- |
| Great teacher/institutional responsibility/autonomy. | Little teacher/institutional responsibility/autonomy. |
| Little centralization/standardization. | Great centralization/standardization. |
| Contextual variation recognized | Contextual variation minimized |

Both the above situations represent movements between two extreme points on a continuum of how national education systems may be organized. The endpoints might be characterized as:

Few education systems anywhere are fully at either end of the continuum, and although situations 1 and 2 both represent a shift from one end to the other, not all educational changes are so extreme. However, the situations do highlight some key features of national-level educational change that need to be borne in mind whatever the degree of movement along the above continuum they may represent. These are that large-scale educational changes:

- are often the result of political and/or ideological change at national government level, and are therefore often decided on very hurriedly
- may represent a major change to established ways of thinking about and carrying out teaching and learning
- affect a large number of people both inside and outside educational institutions
- depend on the attitudes and behaviour of a large number of people both within and outside educational institutions for their successful implementation

All of which mean that such changes:

- are almost always very complex to plan, lead and implement

In the rest of this book I will try to untangle some of the complexity and suggest some key questions that local/institutional leaders can ask – and use the answers to – when planning the implementation of either a locally agreed change or a local version of a national change. First though it is necessary to find out more about 'educational change' itself.

# Chapter 1

# What is educational change?

I think that the question 'what is educational change?' can be divided into four further questions:

1. Why do people decide that they want to change aspects of an education system?
2. What do they hope to achieve by doing so?
3. What is educational change like?
4. What do change-planners and leaders need to consider if they are to be able to support those involved in making change implementation a success?

Below I deal briefly with each of these, discussing the last two together.

## 1.1 Why change?

Planning and implementing a large-scale educational change is not at all easy. Why then might policy makers want to go to the trouble of doing so. One important reason is suggested by the following quote:

> Educational institutions serve both as sites for the perpetuation of society (the stability thesis) and as sites for the changing, developing and creating of society (the improvement of society thesis). (Hunter and Benson 1997: 96)

If educational institutions are sites for the perpetuation or change of society, then one reason for dramatic educational changes such as those represented by situations 1 and 2 above might be that the changes are thought to be needed to support desirable wider changes in other aspects of society as a whole. Why then might such wider changes be considered necessary?

One reason for initiating change that seems to be felt in many national contexts today is linked to the technological and economic effects of globalization. These effects lead national governments to perceive a need to develop policies that will maintain or improve their national competitiveness in a rapidly changing global market place. Existing education systems in many countries have, until recently, continued to provide their citizens with the knowledge traditionally needed to enter a fairly predictable and stable range of lifetime 'employment opportunities'. Such systems are now beginning to be seen as no longer adequate to prepare citizens for life and work in a new 'knowledge age' (Bereiter and Scarmadalia 1998), in which knowledge rapidly changes and becomes out of date. Education systems today therefore need to prepare learners for a world in which knowledge is continuously being expanded, and in which citizens will need to know how to continuously update their knowledge, and how to 'use' what they know flexibly in a range of different work environments. Educational change in such a context may be seen as an important means of enabling the nation to 'keep up' with other external changes that are taking place worldwide.

Another reason given for educational change, especially in some parts of the English-speaking world since the 1980s, has been the feeling that the outcomes of education need to be more strictly standardized and measured. The initial impetus for this feeling was ideological and political: a desire by governments committed to cutting personal taxation in countries such as the UK in the 1980s and 1990s, to make institutions and teachers within them more accountable for the way in which (often very large) education budgets are spent. In such contexts the emphasis when initiating educational change was on designing systems to control and standardize the content and process of education, to make it easier to see exactly what the outcomes of education (measured by learners' performance in standardized tests) actually were in any given school.

More or less explicitly connected to the desire to see clear evidence that the money being spent on education does give the desired 'results' may be a further more 'moral' reason for trying to introduce greater standardization. By having clear standards, applied equally in all schools, it is hoped that there will be 'significant, systematic and sustained change that leads to dramatic improvements in learning for all students in all settings' (Caldwell 2004: 423). Such change, it is hoped, will help to lessen the gap between high- and low-achieving schools and learners, and so contribute to equality of opportunity within society.

A final and more cynical reason for the decision to announce educational-change initiatives is that such announcements can provide good headlines for those doing the announcing. While the rhetoric of such announcements may be inspiring, unless they are backed up by visible implementation policies, their outcomes tend to be negative, increasing cynicism among educational professionals who 'have seen it all before'. Goodson (2001: 53) calls such change initiatives *symbolic, triumphalist action* and points out that any triumph is likely to be very short lived.

So far, therefore, I have suggested four possible reasons for initiating large-scale educational change:

1. to enable the national education system to better prepare its learners for a changing national and international reality
2. to make the education system more clearly accountable for the funding it receives

3. to increase equality of opportunity within society as a whole
4. to use the announcement of educational changes for some kind of short-term political advantage

The main reason more or less explicitly given for any particular change will of course affect what it is hoped that the change will do, and I look at this next.

## 1.2 Changes to what?

If the reason for introducing educational change is based upon an idea that citizens need to be taught different ways of thinking and different skills in order to be able to cope with a very different and rapidly changing national and international geo-political and/or socio-economic environment (reason 1 above), the hoped-for change-outcomes may be quite radical. An example of a 'radical' change would be one where the goal of the change is to try to move from an education system in which the desired outcome of teaching and learning has traditionally been seen as the accurate transmission of knowledge (see chapter 3.2), to one in which the hoped-for outcome is to develop learners' ability to acknowledge and understand different points of view, and through thought, interaction and experience, learn how to construct their own, more personal knowledge.

Any such transition process will of course have implications for many aspects of an education system. The very core of education – 'how teachers understand the nature of knowledge and the students' role in learning and how these ideas about knowledge and learning are manifested in teaching and classwork' (Leithwood et al. 2002) – will need to be reconsidered. Teachers will need to be helped to get to know, and be able to work with, new ways of thinking about knowledge, the teaching–learning process, and teacher–learner roles in that process. There will need to be a move away from the idea that education involves all learners being taught the same 'knowledge' in the same way, towards, for example, a recognition of possible differences between how learners learn (learner styles), what learners bring to their learning, and/or what responsibility they should be encouraged to take in their own learning (learner autonomy). Teaching approaches that are thought to help learners to learn and know in different ways will need to be introduced. Teaching materials and methods of assessment will be affected. All of these will somehow need to be linked and connected into a coherent curriculum document and a coherent plan to guide and support the change process. Inevitably this process will involve many different people. I did say educational change was complex!

Conversely, if the change is in response to a feeling that there needs to be a move towards a more closely monitored system (reasons 2 and perhaps 3 above), in which there is a much more centralized standardized curriculum and more regular national standardized assessment against which teachers' and schools' performance can more easily be measured, this too will affect the education system as a whole. Curriculum documents outlining standards, teaching materials and approaches regarded as necessary to achieve standards, and assessment methods to measure whether standards have been met, will all need to be planned, designed and agreed upon. Teachers will need to be helped to fully understand the standards and targets expected of learners at different levels of assessment, and to become familiar with new materials and/or teaching approaches. National, local and institutional systems to monitor teacher and institutional performance will need to be established. Again a whole range of people in different roles will need to work together.

I am sure you can see that implementing such major changes in education is not just a matter of thinking that it would be a good idea to change, drawing up the necessary documents and then telling teachers to get on with it. So what then are some main characteristics of educational change?

## 1.3 The 'nature' of educational change

One thing I can say for certain is that educational change does not become visible in classrooms directly as a result of a written policy document. Instead, whether it occurs, and what form it ultimately takes, depends on how people understand what is written down and how they behave in response to that understanding. As Fullan (2001: 70) points out, one reason for the failure of so many change initiatives is that policy makers forget this fundamental point.

> Many attempts at policy and programme change have concentrated on product development, legislation and other on-paper changes in a way that ignored the fact that what people did or did not do was the crucial variable.

A way of thinking about the relationship between the official change documentation and actual change that I find helpful is to regard what is written as:

> . . . a musical score – the final effects do not depend just on the score, but on the expertise and skills of the interpreters. (Farias 2000: 2)

If educational change is dependent on how people interpret and act upon the written official 'score', then what does that mean in practice? I will take the hoped-for outcomes of change discussed at 1.2 as examples, and think about what would need to happen for there to be visible changes in classrooms.

First, in either example there needs to be a degree of what Fullan (2007) calls 'reculturing' of the people most closely involved (teachers and those responsible for change planning and implementation). By reculturing I mean that it would first be necessary for these people to begin a process of adjusting many of their established professional (and possibly personal) behaviours, and eventually also beliefs about their roles and responsibilities. This is easy to say, but in fact very few people (including the author) find it easy to 'reculture' (change their long-standing professional behaviours or beliefs) quickly.

This truth leads us to a second feature of educational change: The more ambitious and demanding the change is, in terms of its scale, and especially in terms of the degree of difference it hopes to bring about in what happens in classrooms, the longer it will take. Exactly how long is difficult to judge. Fullan (2007), using examples of change mostly from North America, suggests that a large-scale change may take 5–10 years to become part of normal classroom life in the majority of schools. Birzea (in Polyzoi et al. 2003) suggests that there are other contexts, such as those typical of education systems in many countries of East and Central Europe in the 1990s, where the depth of the reculturing process needed to make changes of the kind discussed in 1.2 may take a generation to achieve. Berend (2007), focusing on the same region, believes it takes even longer. Referring to social transformation, which I believe to be very similar to the reculturing that much educational change entails, he says:

> Social transformation, including the adoption of a new value system and social behavioral pattern, is not a process of one or two decades. It takes generations. (280)

Whichever view we take, it is clear that the successful implementation of educational change takes a long time. It is an ongoing process, not an event that takes place at a particular point in time. This implies that if a large-scale and culturally challenging educational change initiative is not to become merely a further example of 'symbolic triumphalist action', the time scale needed for implementation means that the change needs to be seen as a national, not a government, issue (Cox and Le Maitre 1999). The change process will continue to need economic and political support over what may be a decade or more, and this can only happen if governments 'put educational investment beyond their own need for political survival' (Fullan 2001: 233). Examples of such governments are unfortunately rare.

The process of planning and implementing educational change therefore needs to be viewed as a medium- to long-term process whose success, in terms of real changes to the outcomes of student learning, may demand significant changes to participants' classroom practices and beliefs. While ultimately people's beliefs strongly influence their behaviour, people often find it difficult to talk about their professional beliefs to others without reference to actual practices. Any systems developed to support the many people involved in a change process therefore need to be able to provide participants with opportunities to experience new behaviours in action. Only when people have experienced these, and (hopefully) seen some evidence that persuades them that these do result in better outcomes (however defined), will they seriously question their pre-existing beliefs. Belief change therefore is usually a result of noticing visible positive effects of change; it is *not* a cause of them. Some ideas about how opportunities to experience new behaviours might be provided will be discussed in section three of the book.

I have said that for almost any large-scale educational change that hopes to lead to visible differences in actual classrooms, all people involved will need a greater or lesser degree of 'reculturing' (see chapter 3.2). It is important for policy makers and educational leaders at all levels of the system to try to understand what this expectation might mean to people, and how they might react. For me, and perhaps for you too, being expected to change our existing visible professional behaviours (and eventually the less visible assumptions/beliefs on which they are based) is potentially threatening, because it may affect other familiar aspects of our daily (working) lives. For example, if you or I try to change our longstanding, familiar, forms of professional behaviour for the different practices that an educational change introduces, our existing working relationships with learners, colleagues, superiors, and possibly also parents and figures in the wider society, may all be affected. These professional relationships matter (Hargreaves 1998). They contribute to our sense of professional and personal success and satisfaction. If I am not appropriately supported through the change process, I may experience it as an attack on my 'key meanings' (Blackler and Shinmin 1984); my day-to-day perceptions of myself and of my relationships with others that provide me with important personal and professional stability and security. Since the success of an educational change depends centrally on whether people are willing to play an active role in helping it happen, it is essential to consider how the process may make them feel.

The following quote has appeared in all four editions of the book from which it comes (Fullan's *The (New) Meaning of Educational Change*). The first edition was published in 1981. The fact that he finds it necessary to repeat it in his 2007 edition suggests that its message has not yet been fully understood.

> Neglect of the phenomenology of change – that is how people actually experience change as distinct from how it might have been intended – is at the heart of the spectacular lack of success of most social reforms. (Fullan 2007: 8)

Planning and implementing educational change therefore needs to take people's feelings into account. Apart from any potential psychological/emotional threats to peoples' professional (and personal) self-perceptions, the process of 'reculturing' involves developing confidence in new practices and this demands ongoing investment of additional time and energy from participants. If people are to feel that their ongoing investment in change implementation is worthwhile, given that in most national contexts those working in education already work long hours for less than spectacular wages, the manner in which the change process is planned and implemented is clearly extremely important.

I imagine that by now you can see that any change planning and implementation process is potentially complex. The complexity in any particular context will depend on the extent to which the change represents a challenge to the existing educational reality in that context. It is therefore unlikely that there can be any universal blueprint or template for the educational change process. Although this is so, attempts have been made to classify approaches to the process. One of the most commonly cited classifications of approaches to planning changes in human systems (which education systems most definitely are) dates back to Chin and Benne (1969). I paraphrase it here, adding my own comments.

Chin and Benne suggest that there are three main approaches. The first they call the rational empirical approach. This starts from the belief that people are rational beings. It assumes that they will therefore respond positively to any expected change for which there is well articulated and persuasive (research-based) evidence to show that participating in the change is more or less directly in their own self-interest. Of course I know, and I am sure that you would agree, that people are not purely rational beings. In addition, the term 'rational' is in itself subjective, since what may appear completely rational to me may not appear so to you. Consequently, perceptions of self-interest, in any plan for an educational change that will affect large numbers of people, are therefore likely to vary greatly, regardless of the 'weight' of the evidence offered.

The next they call a normative-re-educative approach. This is based on the idea that most people are influenced by the attitudes and behaviours of other members of their peer group. If they see that their peers have changed their behavioural norms, they will change their own to conform to the new 'changed' group norms. This may often be true, but this approach does not explain how to deal with the fact that for this process to take place, there first needs to be a critical mass of peers (Markee 1997) suggests 5–25 per cent of potential adopters committed to the change process) who have already adopted the new norms. The planning process therefore has to develop a means of generating such a critical mass before this approach can be expected to work for the majority of change participants.

Chin and Benne's final approach is called the power-coercive approach. I feel that many of you will be as familiar with it and its effects as I am. This approach takes a very top-down view of the change process. Those who have the power within the system, organization or institution being changed (the national policy makers and their local representatives) plan the change with little, or usually no, consultation with those whom it will affect. They then present the change documents to those lower down the hierarchy as something that must be implemented (often immediately or with very little notice), with stated or unstated sanctions or threats if their expectations are not met.

Although some of the ideas emerging from these approaches are useful (making the benefits of change as clear as possible to those who will be affected, or trying to make sure that enthusiastic early participants have the opportunity to encourage and support more doubtful ones), none of them alone provide a solid model for the complex process of planning and implementing large-scale educational change.

This has been quite a dense section of reading. So to summarize, I consider some important features of educational change to be that:

- its success depends not on what is written but on how people interpret and act upon what is written
- it is a medium- to very long-term process
- it needs to be separated from politics
- it can make great professional (and personal) demands of people
- it can, to begin with at least, make people feel professionally or personally unconfident
- implementation requires the investment of a great deal of time and effort by large numbers of individuals
- people are more likely to feel that they wish to make this effort if they can see some evidence that the new practices have, or are likely to have, positive outcomes

These then are some of the features that need to be borne in mind by those planning and implementing educational change at any level, if the hoped-for classroom changes and (usually) eventual wider social changes are to become visible.

Although there is no uniform template of how to carry out an educational-change process, the educational-change literature tends to divide the process into several chronologically linear stages. This is a simplification because in practice educational change involves so many different people in so many different contexts that the boundaries of each stage are rarely completely clear and there is often a great deal of moving backwards and forwards between them. In naming them I have borrowed most terms (although not always their exact definitions) from Fullan (2007).

The first stage of an educational-change process, which I will call initiation (other common names are 'adoption' and 'mobilization'), is mostly a thinking and discussing stage. It is the period during which the idea of change is first raised, and when issues like whether it is really necessary, whether it is affordable and/or politically desirable and what form implementation might take are likely to be discussed. If changes never get beyond this stage, few people hear of them. However, if a decision is made to go ahead with some agreed change(s), an active planning and implementation stage follows. This tries to map out plans for the first few years of trying to introduce the practices that the change hopes to see in classrooms. Due to failures of various kinds at the planning stage, the implementation of many educational changes never really takes place as anticipated, or is abandoned, before reaching the final stage of the process.

This last stage is called continuation, routinization or institutionalization, and as these names imply, it refers to the point at which the change is no longer seen to be 'new' and 'different', but has instead become a more or less accepted and unremarkable part of 'how things are done' in most classrooms across the existing system. In my experience, few large-scale educational changes fully reach this final stage in the tidy and uniform manner that many policy documents suggest that it will. Instead, as will be seen in chapter 3, where this final stage is reached, many versions of the original changes are likely to have been developed to meet the needs of different classrooms across the country.

In the next chapter I discuss some important issues that need to be considered at the first stage of any educational process, the initiation or 'thinking about' stage.

# Chapter 2

# Initiating educational change

When national policy makers perceive a need for change, perhaps for one of the reasons at 1.2 above, there are three interrelated factors that I feel it is essential to think about during any discussion of what form the change should take and how it might be implemented.

## 2.1 Starting where people are

An educational change involves people. Some of the people are listed in the quote below.

> Teachers, children and parents all need to adjust their beliefs as well as their behaviours if they want to satisfy the curriculum. In addition educational leaders need to modify their beliefs so that they could accept the new teaching and learning ways. (Zeng 2005: 10)

If, as the quote suggests, the success of an educational change depends on what people do and think, it makes sense to start any discussion of what a desired change is likely to involve by considering the practices and ideas about education that are already familiar to the people who will be affected by the change, what the strengths and weaknesses of these are and whether the proposed change can build on them. One way of beginning this process is to take what Tudor (2003) calls an ecological perspective and consider the existing factors that influence what 'people' (teachers, learners, educational administrators and even parents) believe about education, and so what roles and behaviours they expect of each other and of themselves.

QUESTION TO CONSIDER
What does the quote below suggest that parents believe about education, learning and teaching?

'Every day they [parents] would usually expect their children to learn some specific things at school and show them at home. Otherwise they would question the teaching quality of the teachers or the school.' (Zeng 2005: 20)

I feel that this shows that parents:

- understand the content of education as consisting of specific visible items of knowledge
- expect these items to be taught incrementally, with some new and different items added each day
- judge the ability of a teacher by whether they teach a steady stream of such items
- see learning as involving writing the items down
- judge learning by what has been written down
- see a 'good school' as one in which teachers provide a regular supply of new items to be learned

The educational reality in any context, however similar or different it may be to that outlined above, needs to be the starting point for discussion of what change to introduce and how to introduce it, since it represents the day-to-day setting into which it will be introduced. If policy makers ignore existing local practices and beliefs when deciding on the content and process of change, it immediately makes it very unlikely that the change will ever reach the institutionalized stage of becoming an accepted and normal aspect of most classrooms.

So how can policy makers become aware of people's reality, and ideally also enable representatives of those who will be affected to understand their own thinking about, and hopes for, change? The answer seems obvious: by talking to them and closely observing their reality! However, this rarely seems to happen, since in most (if not all countries) the education system remains extremely hierarchical. Very broadly, 'people' working at 'primary' level are at the bottom of this hierarchy and people working in the better known, older universities are at the top. In addition most policy making continues to be top down, using some version of a power-coercive approach. Where policy makers do talk to anyone, it tends to be to 'education experts' who, in a hierarchical system, are usually assumed by policy makers to be clustered in universities. It may be many years since these 'experts' have had personal experience of the national school system. Consequently they may often be as detached from the realities of the local classrooms into which new practices are to be introduced as the policy makers themselves.

Limited consultation with a narrow range of academic 'experts' continues to be a common scenario despite widely disseminated research (see suggested further reading at the end of this section), suggesting that policy makers need to consult as fully as possible about the content of, and implications for teaching and learning of, any proposed changes with those who will be affected (institutional leaders, local educational administrators and teachers). These people are likely to number tens or hundreds of thousands, so how might consultation happen in practice?

One idea that I like is adapted from Goodson (2003). He suggests that the teaching profession can be divided into three broad groups: 20 per cent whom he calls the 'elite or vanguard teachers', the most creative and committed teachers; a further 60–70 per cent of 'mainstream or backbone teachers'; and a final 10–20 per cent of 'borderline teachers'. I believe that this same rough division could be used for teachers in more or less any country worldwide, and that it also holds approximately true for other key participants in any educational-change process such as institutional leaders and local educational administrators. Goodson suggests that representatives of the 'vanguard' teachers (and I would add vanguard 'other people' also) should be involved in discussions at the initiation stage. I agree fully, especially in terms of ensuring that policy makers obtain a broadly representative sense of existing educational reality. One possible means of involving as wide a sample as possible would be for policy makers to hold structured discussions at local/regional levels, whose conclusions would genuinely be considered during final discussions at the national level. Alternatively, interaction between the policy makers and people, to identify important features of the existing situation that might influence the type of change and the implementation approaches that would be appropriate, could be carried out more formally through an official formal systematic investigation of the existing status quo, sometimes called a baseline study.

However formal or otherwise such a 'baseline study' may be, its value will be dependent on two factors. The first is whether policy makers understand the sorts of questions they need to ask to obtain a picture of existing educational reality, and whom to ask them of. The second is whether they are genuinely willing to listen to and act upon the answers (especially those that are not what they wish to hear!). If the wrong questions are asked of the wrong people, and/or if 'wrong' answers are ignored because they do not 'fit' preconceived plans, the process will be valueless. This very process of genuinely trying to find out what existing realities are, and taking these into account in deciding on what change to introduce and how to introduce it, will, in many top-down education systems, itself be a sign of significant 'reculturing' among policy makers.

Questions to ask, some possible answers and suggestions of how to use answers to inform local-level change planning and implementation processes, will be discussed in more detail in section 3 Here I provide just a few obvious examples of variables that policy makers might need to consider in most educational contexts, in order to identify institutional and individual 'readiness' for, or 'fit' with, the hoped-for outcomes of a proposed change:

1. Class sizes.
2. Teaching and learning resources available in most classes.
3. Availability of sufficient appropriate teaching materials.
4. Content and format of existing high-stakes assessment systems.

5. Level and type of training received by most teachers – their existing strengths and how these match proposed new practices.
6. Existing perceptions of in-service teacher development/support and the availability of functioning structures for providing it.
7. Teacher educators' current strengths and understanding of the proposed change, and hence their readiness to support teachers in developing confidence in new practices.
8. Cultural assumptions among educational administrators, school leaders and the wider public (parents) about teaching, learning, the roles of teachers and learners.
9. Cultural assumptions about how schools should work as organizations in terms of, for example, relationships between leaders and 'led', and/or assumptions about sharing information.

I see (1) to (3) and (5) to (9) above as representing examples of two different aspects of any contextual reality. The former group represent aspects that are concrete and so easily and quickly visible. Some of them can also be changed quite quickly, provided funding is available. For example, if an aspect of a change relates to greater use of technology in classrooms, the necessary hardware and software could, at a cost, be bought and installed quite quickly (whether or how it would be used is another matter). The latter aspects relate to people – how they behave and think. Changes to people's behaviours and, especially, beliefs are less immediately visible and take far longer. However, if (5) to (9) do not change to 'fit' change aims, any money spent on the visible aspects of the context, (1) to (3), will be largely wasted. In my experience many educational changes fail to achieve their aims because policy makers over-emphasize quickly visible concrete changes (for example the introduction of computers into schools worldwide) and underestimate the importance of changes in people.

You will notice that I have not mentioned (4). Although it is a very visible aspect of any education system, there are numerous examples (especially in English language education) of an apparent blindness among policy makers when it comes to ensuring that the content and format of high-stakes assessments 'fit' the changes in teaching content and/or approach that they are trying to implement across the education system. This may be because in many education systems high-stakes exams play an important social and political gate-keeping role, effectively determining whether a learner has access to a 'good' secondary school or university, and any changes to exams are therefore potentially very sensitive. However, if people in a change context (parents, learners, teachers, institutional leaders) see an obvious lack of harmony between the behaviours/practices underlying the proposed changes and those that are perceived to help learners pass high-stakes exams, it is the practices that support success in assessment that will 'win'.

## 2.2 Identifying and communicating the 'need for change'

Large-scale educational changes are usually very time consuming and very expensive. They involve a degree of disruption to many people's lives. If they are to be accepted, they need to meet a clearly visible educational need, so that their rationale can be clearly communicated to all those likely to be directly or indirectly affected. Preceding and parallel to identifying people's existing educational realities, the discussions at the initiation stage therefore also need to seriously consider why change is needed, what the hoped-for outcomes are, what forms the changes should take, and how to communicate all of these to the many different groups of people who will have a more or less direct role in planning and carrying out the implementation process.

To recap 1.2, the most commonly occurring reasons underlying a perceived need for large-scale educational change can be summarized as being to:

- ensure that the manner in which citizens are educated will help the nation remain competitive in a rapidly changing wider international political, economic and technological environment
- standardize the content and process of education in order to enable greater accountability through objective measurement of individual and institutional performance and progress
- better ensure genuine equality of opportunity and so enhance social stability
- deflect attention from other (probably short-term political) issues or problems

If learners and parents are included among those affected by national educational change, it is probably true to say that national educational changes affect a majority (or at least a very large minority) of any population. Consequently, to be able to justify the launch of such a complex, long-term, expensive and potentially disrupting process, policy makers need to have considered how to explain it to people at a range of different levels in a convincing manner.

Once a decision to proceed with the change has been taken, an important part of the initiation process will therefore be to agree how to raise awareness of the change among those who will sooner or later feel its effects. Different levels of detail and different means of communication may be appropriate for different groups of people. However, since the change process takes such a long time, if it is ever to become institutionalized, it is extremely important to establish initial awareness of, and social consensus about, the need for and desirability of change. Shared consensus among such a large proportion of the population will provide a bedrock of support for all those actively involved, once the implementation stage begins. Conversely, lack of at least some understanding of the change among the different affected groups will only increase the complexity of implementation.

This need for wide communication of the change again highlights the desirability of involving representatives of people from all affected levels of the education system from the very beginning of the initiation process. The wider the range of representatives involved at this stage, the easier it will be to communicate the change appropriately at different levels. I will say more about the need for good communication in the next chapter.

## 2.3 Making a long-term commitment

If discussions about the need for change, and what form it should take, are as wide-ranging as I have suggested, they will take time to complete. This will be the first stage of the educational change to need funding. It will also be the stage at which future funding commitments for the agreed change time scale will need to be made. Assuming a decision to proceed with the change is eventually taken, the decisions made about the two issues of time and money will make a huge difference throughout the implementation stage. In 1.3 I suggested that large-scale changes would take upwards of five years of consistent effort to become institutionalized. I also mentioned that for such consistent effort to be possible, policy makers need to consider a large-scale educational-change project as a national rather than a political responsibility, when agreeing on time scales and funding. The implementation stage of the change process will be seriously undermined if initiators have not committed themselves to funding the change over a realistic time span, and agreed how funding and responsibilities will be divided between national and local implementers.

Given that they are the funders and the initiators of change, national policy makers will almost always wish to maintain an overview of how the change process is progressing. Their responsibilities may take the form of a continuous change-monitoring role, coupled with a role in agreeing on any policy adjustments to be made in the light of the evidence of greater or lesser progress emerging from such monitoring. They may also wish (or need) to play a role in ensuring materials or high-stakes assessments are adjusted, or in the provision of appropriate professional development support for local administrators, teacher educators, teachers and their leaders. Whatever roles policy makers choose to retain centrally, funding needs to be allocated to enable them to carry them out over the many years of the process.

The local planning, supporting, monitoring and institutional adjusting that make up actual implementation in schools and their classrooms will of course take place in a range of more or less different local and institutional environments. One means of making it almost certain that the change implementation stage will be viewed unenthusiastically at a local level is to obviously under-resource it. If funds to support the local planning and implementation process over time are insufficient, local educational leaders have limited choices. While they can always 'borrow' funds allocated to other areas of their responsibility to subsidize the change implementation process, this will make them unpopular with those affected by cuts to other budgets. Overall though, serious shortage of funding will only further complicate an already complex process and if funding is simply not available local leaders may well decide to abandon part of the implementation effort or simply give up completely, thus wasting most of the human and financial investment that has already taken place.

Decisions made at the initiation stage will have far-reaching consequences for the experiences of a great number of people. The next chapter supposes that policy makers have made the decision to introduce a large-scale educational change. It discusses some issues, relevant to leaders at all levels, that will influence the route that implementation takes, and the rate at which/extent to which versions of proposed change practices becomes visible in a majority of most classrooms.

# Chapter 3

# The implementation stage

Educational change depends on what a whole range of people who are more or less directly involved actually do. If they are to do what the change expects them to do, a degree of 'reculturing' is often needed. Within any national education system, people work in differing contexts. If all of this is true, the starting point for change implementation at any level must, I feel, include making decisions about:

- what new practices (based on what new 'beliefs) the national change documents wish to 'see'
- what challenges these changes pose for people's (not just teachers') existing practices and beliefs
- whether the new change practices will need to be adapted to 'fit' the existing context
- what support people will need to become able to change their practices appropriately
- what information about the change needs to be communicated to whom, and how to do this
- what systems need to be set up locally to monitor the change process

The people most obviously and directly affected by the changes in practice that most educational changes demand are teachers. However, teachers' experiences of the change implementation process will be influenced, for better or worse, by the behaviour of many others within their local educational environment, including:

- **Local educational leaders/civil servants** – representatives of the national educational policy makers. They may hold the local funding for the change process and are responsible for leading and managing the change process within their administrative area. The extent to which they recognize how national documents will need to be adjusted to match local contextual realities, the need to communicate the change within their area and the need to appropriately support teachers, may all affect teachers' implementation experiences more or less positively.

- **Institutional leaders** – responsible for leading and managing change in their schools. They are probably fund holders for any change budget allocated to individual institutions. The extent to which, and manner in which, they communicate with their teachers, and the efforts that they are willing to make to try and ensure that the school environment is supportive to teachers' attempts to adjust their practices, will directly affect their teachers.
- **Teacher educators** – responsible for providing teachers with formal and informal opportunities to develop the understandings and abilities needed to begin to try out new practices in their classrooms. Their own understanding of the changes and what they imply for teachers' practices, together with their professional understanding of how teachers' learn, will critically influence the value of the support they are able to give.
- **Colleagues** – who may also be trying to implement new practices (unless the change applies to only some curriculum subjects) can be an important sources of day to day support to each other.
- **Learners** – may be having to learn new ways of behaving 'as a learner', and their attitude towards having to do so can be more or less helpful for their teachers.
- **Parents and the wider community** – may have to adjust some of their expectations about what their children do in school. Their attitude is likely to influence their children's (learners') attitudes, and so indirectly affect teachers and institutional leaders.

All of these people have more or less active roles to play in the implementation process. The greater the consistency in the manner in which they approach their own aspects of the process, the more likely it is that teachers will feel that they are adequately prepared and supported, and so feel willing and able to try to do their best in the classroom.

## 3.1 Matching change to local realities

Although I have said that most large-scale change processes remain top down, their implementation is not a neat, rational and uniform process of simply using the resources that have been made available to apply the change practices identically in every school. How could it be when so many different people in so many different places are involved? Institutions in any national education system vary. This means that even where policy makers invest in consulting/communicating widely at the initiation stage on the need for change and the form it should take, and in identifying important features of the educational reality into which it will be introduced, classroom outcomes will not be identical.

Schools may vary due to their geographical location (close to or far from the main population centres, with good or poor transport links) or due to local socio-economic factors (the prosperity or poverty resulting from growing or declining sources of employment). They may vary in terms of the cultural homogeneity of their learners, who may represent one or several or many cultural backgrounds. Such variations may affect perceptions of the value of education among parents, the types of teachers and school leaders that the area attracts and manages to keep, and the class sizes and quality of educational infrastructure that are commonly found. Any combination of these may affect the extent and/or type of 'reculturing' that implementation of a national educational change entails. This makes it highly likely that local change leaders will need to adjust aspects of national change policy to make it appropriate for local implementation.

If this is so, what does this suggest about the nature of change implementation? First, it suggests that it is not a uniform process. It looks different in different places. It is carried out at different speeds. It is carried out to differing degrees of conformity to the official documents. So its ultimate outcomes will look different. There is nothing that can be done about this. As a result, if the education system as a whole is to benefit from the implementation process, national policy makers need to explicitly encourage local leaders to begin their implementation stage by introducing a version of the change that is true to the 'spirit' of what is being attempted while also being appropriate for the majority of their schools. I believe that taking such a flexible approach makes it more likely that more change will be visible in more classrooms than will be the case if all contexts are pressured to implement the new practices identically. To begin with, some change is better than none, and trying to force a square peg into a round hole cannot work.

How then can a national change be adjusted to 'match' a local reality? What factors need to be considered? I return again to the idea of coherence and the need for harmony between the proposed change and the change situation into which it is to be introduced. In most countries, local representatives of the national education authorities are likely to be responsible for planning and managing the implementation process in their own area. If there has been insufficient consultation and communication at the initiation stage, they themselves may of course not fully understand what the change is trying to achieve. Even where they do understand the reasons for the change and its goals, if there has been no encouragement to interpret these goals as appropriate for their context, they may feel that they have to implement it according to 'the book'. However, assuming that such encouragement has been given, adjustments to local conditions will involve looking at existing material resources and teaching practices and thinking how the change can be adapted to allow implementation to begin in a manner that will reflect at least some of the key principles at the heart of the change. Aspects of the local context that are likely to be relevant include:

- the teachers' current practices – what they are familiar with and do well, which new practices they are likely to find difficult
- class sizes – whether these are likely to make the introduction of some new practices difficult
- resources and teaching materials – whether the new practices require use of particular resources/teaching materials, and whether these are present in most schools or could be provided

- demands of high-stakes assessment – whether the content and format of important national examinations support the introduction of new practices
- provision of teacher development personnel and opportunities – whether local teacher educators understand and will be able to provide appropriate support in the new practices, or whether they will require trainer-training
- awareness of, and a positive attitude to, new practices, and an understanding of their rationales on the part of most institutional leaders
- awareness of, and likely attitude towards, the new practices on the part of the wider society in the area – the parents
- money – how much funding is available for how long to pay for teacher support, resources, adjusting class sizes, etc.

For a variety of historical, geographical and socio-economic reasons, each local context will be at least slightly different in terms of some of the above bullet points. If local change implementers try to match the change to their local context, each such context will initially have its own more or less different version of change being implemented. As discussed above, I believe that this is natural. What matters most for the ultimate achievement of the change aims is that the manner in which the implementation process is carried out in a particular area takes account of the actual daily working realties of those who are expected to introduce and use new practices in local classrooms – most centrally teachers (and their learners). However appropriately change aims are adapted, teachers are almost certain to need support at the beginning of the implementation stage. Means of providing such support are discussed in the next part of this chapter.

## 3.2 Support for learning the what and how of change

If much educational change involves a degree of personal/professional 'reculturing' for many of those affected by the process, then it is important to get a sense of what this term means. All education systems have a 'culture', by which I mean they have a usually longstanding and widely agreed way of thinking about the meaning of terms like 'education' or 'knowledge' or 'teaching' or 'learning'. Simplifying a complex idea, it is possible to conceptualize any educational culture as being situated at a particular point along one or more continua. To illustrate, continua representing four possible characteristics of any educational culture, adapted from Hofstede (1994), are shown in Figure 3.1. Following Young and Lee (1984), I label the two ends of each continuum 'transmission based' and 'interpretation based', but of course as mentioned in chapter 1, few educational cultures are consistently situated at either extreme.

**Figure 3.1** Four possible characteristics of educational culture

| Transmission based | What knowledge is | Interpretation based |
|---|---|---|
| Knowledge is clearly defined and there is one right answer to almost any question. | | Knowledge is dynamic and is arrived at through discussion |
| The purpose of education is to learn knowledge | The purpose of education | The purpose of education is to learn how to learn |
| Learners are members of a group and speak only when spoken to | Learners | Learners are a collection of individuals who are expected to express themselves |
| Teachers are the initiators of classroom activity and should know all the answers | Teachers | Teachers are there to support learners' participation in the learning process and can admit ignorance |

QUESTIONS TO CONSIDER

What might an implementation stage that expected teachers to move from the practices and beliefs typical of a transmission-based culture towards those of an interpretation based culture actually demand of a teacher? What changes to existing ways of thinking and behaving might a teacher need to learn? What support would a teacher need?

New ways of behaving might include:

- using a more varied range of teaching approaches, including ones that involve learners in interaction and discussion
- developing a different classroom atmosphere in which learners feel encouraged to make contributions
- using a wider range of materials that will provide learners with a range of different points of view

In the long run, successful use of such new practices would hopefully result in changes to beliefs that might include recognizing:

- that even though one is a teacher one does not always need to know the answer to everything
- that in a classroom there is more than one right answer to many questions
- that learners can usefully contribute to their own learning

The above changes to behaviour and (eventually) beliefs provide a sense of what reculturing might entail for a teacher trying to implement a complex educational change. Such a reculturing process can, as mentioned in chapter 1, make people feel uncomfortable and concerned about their professional identity. If teachers (and learners) are to be able to 'reculture' in this way they need support from each other, from their institutional leaders and from local educational administrators. I look at some aspects of successful support next.

One feature still common to most educational cultures worldwide is that teachers spend almost all their time alone in their classrooms with their learners and (once qualified) are rarely, if ever, observed teaching by anyone else. Most teachers are not expected to and so are not used to sharing pedagogy. In many contexts they have few regular opportunities to spend time discussing professional issues during their working day. Evidence from educational change contexts suggests that in this respect there needs to be a major reculturing of almost every education system, since the value of sharing, collaboration and team work is repeatedly emphasized in discussions of how teachers can be supported in implementing change.

Developing confidence in new practices takes time. To begin with, most teachers will probably only be able to see the reform goals through the lenses of their existing beliefs and understandings. For example, in a change process that involves a move away from a transmission-based educational culture, participants who are used to thinking of educational knowledge as mainly a series of facts may begin the change implementation process thinking that the change will involve the learning and teaching of new and different facts. For them to move to an understanding that this is not so, and then to develop confidence in their personal ability to behave in a different manner, will be a long-term process. The exact stages of this process will be different for each individual. However, for teachers, simply put, in some form or another it probably involves:

(a) developing a deep understanding of what the change aims mean for classroom practice and why they are worth introducing
(b) using their current level of understanding (with or without more expert help) to plan how to introduce new practices
(c) trying out new practices with learners in a classroom
(d) seeing what happens when doing so – obtaining explicit or implicit feedback from learners, colleagues or a more expert 'coach' (Joyce and Showers 1988)
(e) going through many more cycles of (a) to (d), slowly developing a more complete personal understanding and personal confidence in practice through carrying it out again and again

These simple words of course hide just what a difficult process 'changing' really is. In addition, the above simple sequence stands a much better chance of working if other important people in the change process (administrators, school leaders and teacher educators) are simultaneously following a similar sequence and have appropriate opportunities to:

- share understandings of the changes as they affect their roles and settings
- receive more or less formal help in planning the leadership/management of implementation (see section 3)

- try out their plans with the people for whom they are responsible
- remain alert and open to available feedback from inside and outside the classroom

Harvey (1999), looking at teachers trying to implement a new model of teaching science in their own classrooms in South Africa, suggested these teachers needed at least 20–25 supported cycles at (b) to (d) above to develop confidence in carrying out practices that represented a change of only medium complexity. He noted that throughout this time their commitment to the change was not very strong and if support was not available they were always likely to revert to their pre-existing practices. In Harvey's case an educational 'expert' provided one-to-one support. Such intense support is unlikely to be available for so many practice cycles in most implementation contexts, but the acknowledgement of the need does help explain the recent rise in the perceived usefulness of mentoring schemes in educational change contexts. Given that people and the contexts that they work in are so different, it is not possible to quantify exactly how much support people need. It is though clear that the greater the reculturing, the longer support will be needed for.

The form that support for teachers takes matters greatly. This is particularly true of any formal training provided, since such training usually happens only once and does not last for long. Situation 3 below is an example of a formal change implementation support attempt that I was responsible for providing many years ago when (as I now know) I knew very little:

Situation 3

*A new language-teaching textbook was about to be launched in a broadly transmission-based educational culture. It was significantly different from the textbooks that were currently in use. It claimed to enable learners to develop their communication skills in the language, especially listening and speaking. It stressed the need to provide learners with opportunities to interact and so used a lot of group and pair work, emphasized the encouragement of fluency rather than being constantly concerned with accuracy, encouraged teachers to make their own choices about the order in which they used (or even whether they used) the various activities, and assessed performance through 'communicative tests'. The existing language-learning materials that teachers were familiar with were reading based and emphasized total comprehension through the sentence-by-sentence study of each sentence's grammar and vocabulary.*

*To introduce teachers to the new materials, a two-week training programme was provided. This spent a lot of time explaining the theory behind the approach taken in the materials. It introduced teachers to the very detailed teachers' book, and the trainer used materials from the book to demonstrate some of the new pedagogic practices that teachers using the book would need to develop. Teachers were then each given a chance to teach a very short part of a unit from the book themselves in front of their colleagues and the tutors and received feedback. They then went back to their institutions where they were supposed to start to use the new books.*

QUESTIONS TO CONSIDER

Have you ever participated in any capacity in a similar short training course that aimed to prepare teachers to implement a change in their classrooms? If you have, do you feel it was successful? What affected how successful it was?

Do you see any weaknesses in the above training course, in terms of its ability to support teachers' understanding of, and confidence in, implementing new practices?

I feel that the main weaknesses include the following:

- the course was not balanced in the time it spent on 'theory' and 'practice'
- the training made no attempt to find out 'where the teachers are now' – to identify their existing practices and beliefs, and the contexts that they worked in, and to use these as a starting point to discuss the new practices
- the teachers had no opportunity to practise in their real working environment

I comment on each of these weaknesses here, drawing widely on Malderez and Wedell (2007), which covers most issues raised in far greater detail.

Theory is easier to teach than to practice. Talking about the academic rationale for the change allows trainers to adopt the lecture mode that is often the form of teaching practice that they are most familiar and comfortable with. Using this mode means they can avoid showing that they themselves are perhaps not very confident about the practices they are urging others to use. However, although such behaviour might be more comfortable for trainers, if the figure of 20–25 practice cycles cited above is even approximately right, providing opportunities for participants to see the new practices in action and practise them themselves in their own classrooms or work environments is very important. The design of implementation training programmes needs to try to provide an appropriate balance between telling teachers about change and enabling them to experience it.

Any formal support for change implementation is likely to be fairly short lived. It may last a few days, a week, a few weeks at most. Its impact on participants' understanding of what the change means for them will be a great deal more powerful if it begins by helping people identify some of the existing principles and practices that guide their work and the constraints that affect them, and to compare these to the principles and practices introduced by the change. Personal and contextual issues revealed as possibly hindering the implementation of change practices provide a starting point for trainers and participants to make decisions about how best to use the limited training time. If trainers do not really know what teachers' ideas and concerns are, how can they know whether what they are doing is in fact what teachers will find useful?

Change implementation usually involves people altering aspects of their familiar professional practice. If at all possible, it makes sense for them to begin trying to do so in their normal work setting, since it is here that they will be most concerned about performing well. Real practice opportunities of this kind during a formal training can provide participants with chances to see what happens when they try to implement change in their classroom. The training environment also provides a supportive setting in which to discuss their early implementation experiences with colleagues who are trying to do the same, while still having access to a (hopefully) more expert trainer. This is not to say that all formal support for a change process should be institution based. However, the value of the training outlined in situation 3 would have been greater if the structure of the programme had been designed to enable participants to spend time using the new materials in their own institutions between perhaps two periods of formal training.

Formal training courses are of course just the beginning of a support process. During the early years of an implementation process, teachers (and institutional leaders and administrators) in a particular local or institutional context all need regular opportunities to interact with others in similar roles. Ideally, most of this interaction will be with colleagues having very similar change experiences in their shared institutional context, but ideally people also need chances to meet others trying to carry out the same change in other institutions.

If people need repeated and supported cycles of practice and feedback to develop confidence in new practices, provision needs to be made for such cycles to be provided within their work settings, together with some sort of support. Since one-to-one 'expert' support for every teacher going through a national change process will never be available, most support will have to come from within people's own institutions. These need to become 'professional learning communities' (Fullan 2007) in which there is an atmosphere of shared learning or peer mentoring (Malderez and Wedell 2007, Malderez and Bodoszcky 1999) in how to implement the change practices. In such a community teachers regularly have the opportunity, for example, to meet to discuss their experiences of trying to implement new practices, possibly agree an observation rota, and share strategies and materials. To begin with at least, such meetings need to be focused and led by a facilitator. This person might be a 'vanguard teacher' from within the institution, who (perhaps due to attending a formal training course and having had some training for the mentor-like role) feels that they are clearer about the change aims and practices than most colleagues, or a local teacher educator provided by the local education administrators.

An important responsibility of local implementation planners is therefore to enable such meetings to become an established part of the implementation stage in most institutions. They will also need to be scheduled in school hours, so that they are not perceived as being 'just more extra work'. How long such meetings will be needed for will of course vary, but the atmosphere of sharing and mutual aid during the implementation stage may be something positive that teachers and institutional leaders wish to retain even once the urgent need has passed, in which case this may represent yet another reculturing effect of the change process.

A coherent programme of formal and informal support for teachers' change implementation at local level is unlikely to happen of its own accord. Good change leadership at all levels is critical, and this is discussed next.

## 3.3 Leading (local) change

Whereas 3.2 dealt principally with teachers, here I discuss the role of local-level change leaders, who are likely to be the educational administrators/civil servants charged with managing implementation in their area, and the leaders of the various institutions that they are responsible for. It could be argued that their role at the implementation stage is the most difficult of all. After all, they are expected both to lead and support others (teachers) through an educational reculturing process, and to simultaneously reculture elements of their own organization and/or their own role, in order to be able to do so.

Leaders need to understand the extent to which their local educational culture 'fits' the classroom behaviours that change implementation implies, in order to be able to decide whether and how national policy needs to be locally adjusted. They also have to consider what the need to develop a 'professional learning community' to support the implementation stage implies for the organizational culture in which they work and for their own leadership practices.

| The management structure of the organization is | | |
|---|---|---|
| A steep hierarchy, with a clearly defined leader and a vertical, top down, chain of command. | | A simple flat hierarchy The leader is first among equals. |
| Staff at lower levels are not expected to show initiative. | _____ | Use of individual initiative and discretion is encouraged. |
| Organization is seen as a number of separate departments. | | Organization is conceived and planned for as a whole. |
| **The organization values staff for** | | |
| Their ability to contribute their specialist knowledge of a particular field to the organisation. | _____ | Their ability to cooperate and share information. Their ability to obtain and act on information gained from internal and external sources. |
| **The organization's attitude to change is to** | | |
| View stability as the norm. Respond slowly to the need for change. Feel uncomfortable with the notion of continuous innovation. | _____ | Assume change and instability to be the norm. Recognize need for, and be keen to, develop the skills to cope with continuous innovation in an unstable world. |

**Figure 3.2**  Some features of organizational cultures (adapted from Wedell 2000)

Organizational cultures, like educational cultures, may be thought of as being situated at points along a range of continua that reflect underlying assumptions about how the organization works and about the roles of the people within it. Figure 3.2 above illustrates what I mean by looking at how three aspects of an organizational culture may vary.

In many contexts, the organizational culture in both local government departments and schools traditionally tends to be towards the left-hand column above. If you think back to the discussion of implementation so far, I hope you will agree that leaders and staff in an organizational culture with these characteristics are unlikely to be flexible enough to cope with the demands of the implementation stage that I have mentioned. Leaders' personal reculturing may therefore be seen as needing to precede that of teachers, since without the development of new leadership practices it may not even be possible to start to provide the supportive environment within which teachers can begin to implement an educational change.

What new practices (and beliefs) do educational leaders who are trying to move the culture of their offices or institutions from a position nearer the left of Figure 3.2 to one nearer the right need to develop? I believe that they include those bulleted below:

- recognizing that change is going to be a long-term (if not permanent) feature of people's daily working life, and that therefore organizational systems need to become more flexible
- developing an organizational atmosphere in which individuals feel encouraged to contribute their ideas about how to support the change process and take personal initiative
- developing new channels of communication within and between schools and offices in order to share the 'burden' of change, and learn from each other's experiences of trying to implement it
- developing ways of helping their staff feel as comfortable as possible with the new administrative, organizational and teaching practices that change will demand
- actively encouraging their staff to cooperate in developing their understanding of and confidence in new practices.

What personal qualities and skills do leaders need to have to be able to successfully support the reculturing of their organization and their staff to meet the unpredictable challenges of an implementation stage? First and obviously they themselves need to fully understand (and hopefully also believe in the value of) the change aims, in order to identify what these mean for their organization, and to be able to help their staff understand and believe in them too. Without such a comprehensive understanding, it will be very difficult for any leader to know how to adjust the detail of the implementation to meet their institutional realities while still retaining the spirit of the change.

However fully a leader understands the change, is able to communicate that understanding and use it to make the expected new practices realistic within the school environment, some teachers are still likely to find reculturing threatening. They have a whole range of possible issues relating to their 'key meanings' (see 1.3) that might worry them: whether they will ever be able to feel as comfortable with the new practices as they do with the existing ones, whether their learners will suffer from their initial unfamiliarity with the new practices, whether their status with parents or their position in the institution or the community will be diminished. Any of these, when added to the extra work that even the best planned and led change implementation entails, may lead teachers to feel that making the effort to change is not worthwhile.

A second important quality for leaders is therefore the need to understand people; to understand that people react differently to change, and that a leader needs to be sympathetic to teachers' anxiety and stress about learning and trying to implement new classroom practices. It is leaders who have to help their staff see that change is achievable, by trying to notice and celebrate individual and group successes. It is leaders who have to help people see that change can offer professional and personal opportunities as well as make demands; opportunities to collaborate with colleagues, to learn to carry out their teaching differently and so refresh their professional life (Oplatka 2005), opportunities to increase professional confidence and satisfaction through the successful implementation of new practices, and most importantly opportunities to have positive effects on learners.

Just as I have argued that national policy makers need to try to maximize involvement in decision making at the initiation stage, so leaders need to try to develop an organizational culture in which change implementation is felt to be a venture that involves everybody (the idea of the professional learning community again). Leaders cannot do everything, so they need to be prepared to delegate, and develop an institutional culture in which it becomes normal for everyone to be involved in decisions about how the change should be implemented and monitored in their institutions, and about whether and how the results of such monitoring should be used to adjust the institutional implementation process. The atmosphere in such an institution will be one in which people who disagree with aspects of implementation, or even of the change practices themselves, will feel confident enough to say so, and know that adjustments will be made to the implementation process if their reasons are agreed to be valid. In such an institutional culture people will be able to feel that they have some control over how the change will affect them.

The leaders' role is central to almost every aspect of implementation. In their own institutions, leaders represent the 'bridge' between a national policy and how it is experienced by implementers – their staff. They have to try and support their staff through their reculturing processes, while at the same time going through their own, and, in many contexts, being expected to provide their superiors with progress reports on their implementation process. They need the self-confidence to cope with the different speeds at which people are able to change their practices, not to panic at the inevitable problems that will arise during the implementation stage, and not to be tempted to hurry teachers along just for the sake of appearing to be changing. They need to be able to cope with lack of certainty, be willing to take responsibility for failures as well as credit staff with successes, and be willing to provide an atmosphere within their institution that supports the collaboration and mutual aid among teachers, which I have said above is an essential feature of supporting change. Few leaders begin any change implementation process with such a wide range of personal and professional qualities already in place.

While it is has long been recognized, however incoherently, that teachers need support in order to change, it is only now beginning to be recognized that change leaders also need support for *their own* reculturing. Since their needs are so wide-ranging, formal training for leaders in educational change contexts remains rare. They (like teachers) do though have one potential source of support available: each other. In addition, therefore, to establishing structures to support teachers and to enable them to support each other, leaders within a local area also need to use some of their funding to set up their own support systems. These can help them to share their understandings of the local change process, and perhaps visit or host visits from leaders at similar levels in other areas to find new information about/discuss problems and solutions for leading implementation.

A local change leader's role is very difficult. They will vary greatly in the speed with which, and the extent to which, they are able to support the implementation stage in the many ways that I suggest they need to. I feel that the most that can be expected is that leaders are seen to be trying to create an environment in which people feel that new practices are supported. That this support may initially be partial and imperfect is, I feel, inevitable.

## 3.4 Implementation: Conclusion

It is impossible to list all the variables that those responsible for leading the local implementation of a large-scale educational change process need to bear in mind. Some of the most important are that:

- the extent of its success depends on the behaviour and attitudes of a very wide range of individuals
- as many of these people as possible need to understand the rationale for, and main aims of, the change to appropriate degrees of detail
- for this widespread understanding to be possible, serious consideration needs to be given to awareness-raising and communication between the various levels of the change process
- people do not respond to change purely rationally, they have feelings, and consequently the implementation process at a national, local or institutional level is almost certain to be unpredictable
- the change practices may need adjusting to meet the realities of local or institutional human and material resources
- the implementation process will last for years. Given its unpredictability, it needs to be monitored at all levels to try to ensure that what is actually happening remains directed towards the spirit of the change aims, while at the same time being practically achievable in a range of different contexts
- given the range of contexts, the implementation process will never be

uniform. It will look different, proceed at different speeds and follow different routes in different institutions

- change often requires a degree of professional reculturing both in terms of approaches to teaching and learning practices, and of the manner in which different levels of organization are led
- the introduction of new practices requires support over time
- the provision of formal and informal support may in turn require formal or informal support for the trainers and leaders whose responsibility it is
- the implementation process therefore needs consistent funding over time
- the new practices need to be in harmony with available teaching and learning materials, and most importantly with national high-stakes assessment

In the light of complicated interrelationships even just among the many variables included in this long list, it will probably not surprise you to read the following:

I can produce many examples of how educational practices could look different, but I can produce few, if any, examples of large numbers of teachers engaging in these practices in large scale institutions designed to deliver education to most children. (Elmore 1995: 11 in Fullan 2007)

The next chapter looks at some of the most common reasons why this is so often the case.

# Chapter 4

# Why educational changes fail

Massive financial and human resources are devoted to trying to improve education worldwide. Some improvements, for example providing access to primary education for a larger proportion of the population, or improving the proportion of the school population who obtain five GCSEs or A grades at A level (taking a UK example), can be quantified. Evidence suggests that improvements whose aim is to offer an existing educational content and process to more people, or to improve how it is offered as measured by learners' performance in high-stakes assessment, can sometimes succeed in meeting their hoped-for outcomes. When they do, the successful change is usually loudly celebrated by educational policy makers and in the media.

In contrast, efforts to try to change the process of what actually happens in classrooms nationwide, with the aim of enabling learners to develop differently and so better meet their educational needs in a rapidly changing world, have usually been far less successful. In this chapter I suggest a number of important reasons for this sad truth, most of which can be traced back to ignorance or lack of care at the initiation stage.

## 4.1 Insufficient understanding of what change is like

The success of any educational change depends on the reactions of a large number of different people in different contexts. However, at the initiation stage when policy makers are making decisions about what changes to try to implement, and how to do so, the tendency remains for change implementation to be viewed as a purely rational process. Too many change initiatives still begin from a position that seems to assume that successful implementation is simply a matter of providing money and resources and implementation plans and saying, 'We expect this change to happen', 'We expect it to happen like this', 'We expect it to begin on this date', and then waiting for the desired change to appear identically in every classroom.

The policy makers and academic 'experts' who are so often the only ones actually involved at the initiation stage still seem to emphasize the technicality of change (Goodson 2003) – the visible resources and systems that need to be available or established – over the 'personality of change', the existing practices and beliefs of all the people who will be affected. This leads to the following 'fundamental strategic flaw':

> The fundamental flaw in most innovators' strategies is that they focus on their innovations, on what they are trying to do – rather than on understanding how the larger culture, structures and norms will react to their efforts. (Senge et al. 1999: 26 in Fullan 2007)

Consequently, in many cases, those involved in initiation continue to believe that their role is merely to draft 'correct' and technically feasible plans for implementing the changes, with little or no need to consider the people who will be carrying them out, or the contexts in which they will be doing so. This simplistic approach to the initiation stage is even more extreme in cases where politicians, looking for quick solutions to educational challenges that they see their own countries facing, decide to just borrow educational change solutions 'off the shelf' from education systems in other countries (Riley 2003), without considering in what ways their educational realities may be different. This tendency has been particularly common in, but not unique to, changes in approaches to English language education over the last two decades or so.

In such initiation situations, where, in the policy makers' eyes, the change documents *are* the change, there is clearly little encouragement to local leaders to be flexible at the implementation stage. In addition, since little effort (beyond transmission of official documents and/or oral presentation) is made to ensure that local-level administrators fully understand what the change is trying to achieve, they are unlikely to feel capable of adjusting change aims to match their local reality. With little or no information about the change other than what is written in the documents, local leaders have little choice but to pass on the 'orders' to the institutional leaders, who, equally unclear, pass them on to teachers to implement. Such a 'communication' process is not supportive for teachers' perceptions of how much their leaders value the change ('The leaders asked us to change because it was a task from the upper leaders. They know no better about the change than the teachers' (Wedell forthcoming)), or for their own understanding of it ('No further and detailed explanation relevant to the change was given by the institutional leadership' (Wedell op. cit.)) In such circumstances the hoped-for new practices are unlikely to find their way into most classrooms.

## 4.2 Blindness to the existing educational culture and teaching-learning conditions

I find it difficult to understand how so many policy makers and their educational experts can remain so blind to their own educational cultures. The focus of their policy making is on introducing change to their education systems. To me this presupposes that a system already exists. However, it often seems that the existing education system and the existing cultural assumptions about education in the wider society remain invisible to policy makers, and so are disregarded in their decision-making.

Consequently, at national level educational-change policy makers and planners often seem able to delude themselves that it is not necessary to think about how the people affected by implementation will react to change, or about how the implementation process might be affected by the existing classroom conditions. Local or institutional leaders are of course much closer to change implementation. If they follow their superiors and ignore local realities, they will find it more difficult to avoid the unsatisfactory outcomes that are likely to follow. Sakui (2004), discussing educational change in Japan, points to some concrete examples of how teachers might be affected by a top-down educational change that makes no concessions to people and places. This change involved a new curriculum with hoped-for outcomes that required the introduction of different practices. Some of the, no doubt unintended, effects on people and practices of an initiation stage that planned change while ignoring existing realities, which were identified by this study, are listed below:

- The change causes teachers to worry, because it expects them to use new practices that require a different classroom management style. Behaviours and interactions typical of this style contradict existing beliefs about the appropriate roles and behaviours of teachers and learners. There may be problems in terms of discipline and noise.
- The change may make it difficult to plan classes to the usual degree of detail because new activities are more open-ended in their outcomes and/or the preparation for such activities is very time consuming. Both the open-endedness and the lack of detailed preparation for each lesson may make teachers (and learners) uneasy.
- The change requires more use of more time-consuming, open-ended, activities. This may make it difficult to adhere to the widespread and longstanding convention that in institutions of a particular type, the textbook for each subject is finished within one academic year, in time for what has been learned in that textbook to be assessed at the end of year. This may lead learners, school leaders and parents to evaluate teachers negatively.
- The introduction of new classroom activities and classroom management styles by teachers who do not feel confident about what they are doing may lead to dissatisfaction among students, school leaders (and their parents) because new practices and classroom activities are not immediately recognizable as 'proper work'.

As I have said repeatedly, in such circumstances, if local administrators and institutional leaders are unable to:

- provide a comprehensible rationale for the change (not just that provided in official documents)

- help teachers see how the practice of the change may be adapted to take account of their classroom realities, while still maintaining (some of) the spirit of the change
- establish systems that provide support for the teachers during the long process of developing confidence in the new practices

then one understandable response for teachers will be to ignore the changes that they are supposed to be implementing and to and carry on as usual.

It is rare to hear of national policy makers seriously investigating reasons why an educational-change initiative does not ultimately lead to any of the hoped-for changes to classroom practises. If they make any public statements at all regarding an unsuccessful change attempt, it is even more rare to hear them admit that reasons for failure have anything to do with their own poor policy making. Instead it is customary to blame teachers for their inability to understand and/or implement new practices. Policy makers' self-delusion continues, nothing has been learned, people working within local education systems become yet more cynical about change initiatives, and any further changes will be welcomed with even less enthusiasm.

## 4.3 Pretending or appearing to change

Given the hierarchical nature of most education systems, it is of course often difficult for teachers or their institutions to completely ignore demands that they should change that come down from higher levels. A common alternative to simply ignoring a change that is felt to be impossible to implement is therefore to simplify the change to the extent that it no longer actually constitutes a change. This may be done by leaders insisting that teachers use the language of change (for example, *learner centred*, *learning strategies*, *communication*) in any public performances and written documents, or that they adopt whatever new materials the change process expects them to use. At a surface level, the institution and the people within it seem to have changed. They may even think themselves that they have changed. They, for example, use the new textbook, which says on the cover that it is learner centred and that it caters for learners' different learning styles, or they use power-point presentations in all their classes. However, if looked at more closely it is clear that the hoped-for aims of the change in terms of practices that might encourage different learning outcomes have barely been touched. Teachers do use the textbook, but they miss out the activities that would involve them in introducing new practices to their classroom, they do use power point, but the content is only the notes they would previously have written on the board.

This state of people appearing to change, or thinking that they have changed, when in fact they have only assimilated some of the jargon and perhaps techniques of change into what they have always done without really understanding why, Fullan has called 'false clarity'. This term too has appeared in the last three editions of his book (1991, 2001, 2007), which again suggests that the phenomenon remains widespread. Claxton notices a very similar phenomenon:

It is not uncommon for example for people to say that they have changed, and even to think that they have changed, but for that change not have affected what they do very much at all. (Claxton 1989: 19)

Whether local leaders or teachers consciously ignore changes that they are expected to implement, or unconsciously assimilate the surface manifestations of the change practices and language into their existing practice, classrooms change very little. Surprisingly, policy makers often appear unconcerned about whether changes have been superficially or more deeply absorbed. The documents at all levels of the system state that change has been introduced, new teaching materials or ways of presenting teaching materials are being used, the illusion of change exists. However, the hoped-for outcomes of the change are not achieved.

## Conclusion to section 1

So what conclusions about educational change is it possible to draw from this section of the book?

Any national educational change will have to take account of a great many interrelated variables in different local environments. I divide them into three broad interconnected categories, whose variables may influence the change process in a particular national or local context to differing degrees at different stages of that process. The categories are:

- the material conditions into which the change is to be introduced. Are they broadly compatible with the behaviours and activities that the change hopes to promote?
- the existing experiences and educational culture of the people whom the change will affect. What degree and manner of reculturing will be needed/is feasible to make actual implementation possible?
- the existing 'organizational culture' of the institutions at every level of the system. What reculturing will be needed for each level to be able to communicate, support and lead the change adequately?

Some variables in each category are shown in Figure 4.1.

How the above variables interact over time within a particular level of an educational setting will affect the rate, route and eventual outcome of the change process. Ideally those leading change implementation will understand how to focus on the right variables at the right time to the right extent for the context that they are working in. Since what is 'right' at one stage of the process may not be so at a different stage, constant monitoring of implementation will be needed together with the confidence to respond flexibly to the information emerging from such monitoring. In most contexts, change leadership training is likely to be needed if leaders are to understand their complex roles.

I have suggested that top-down, largely power coercive, strategies that assume that change implementation will occur merely because national policy makers have

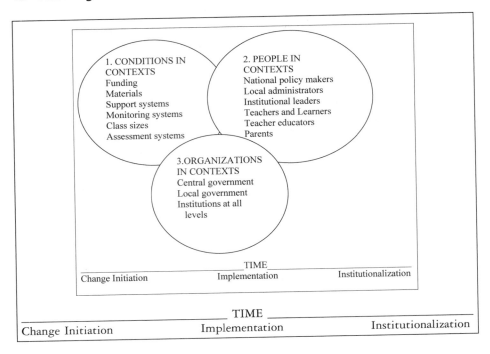

1. CONDITIONS IN
CONTEXTS
Funding
Materials
Support systems
Monitoring systems
Class sizes
Assessment systems

2. PEOPLE IN
CONTEXTS
National policy makers
Local administrators
Institutional leaders
Teachers and Learners
Teacher educators
Parents

3.ORGANIZATIONS
IN CONTEXTS
Central government
Local government
Institutions at all
levels

TIME

Change Initiation      Implementation      Institutionalization

TIME

Change Initiation      Implementation      Institutionalization

decided that it is necessary do not seem to work. What more successful approach to initiation and implementation planning might national policy makers adopt? As suggested in chapter 2.1, a combination of top-down and bottom-up strategies may be an answer.

Such a combination might be imagined as beginning with top-down national policy makers who understand that the decisions that they make about new practices at the initiation and national implementation planning stages will in fact need to be carried out in many local contexts. Policy makers therefore involve representatives of as many different levels as possible in decision making early on, and provide support/training that will enable critical local-change agents (local educational administrators, school leaders and teacher trainers) to develop as full an understanding as possible of how change practices will affect local teachers and schools. When planning for implementation, policy makers support local change leaders in making their own detailed local plans for how to implement the new practices in a manner that takes local contextual variables into account. What might the stages of such a process look like in practice? Table 4.1 suggests an approach that tries to incorporate most of the issues that have been identified as important in this section of the book.

**Table 4.1** One approach to initiating a national educational change

| National policy makers (NPM)<br>National coordinating body (NCB) | Local planners/leaders |
|---|---|
| **CHANGE-INITIATION STAGE** | |
| (a) NPMs begin by agreeing that the change should be seen as a national (not a political) initiative. *All political groups commit to a minimum of ten years of national leadership and funding before a decisive evaluation.* | |
| (b) NPMs recognize the need to fully develop their own understanding of the what and why of the desired change, and of how it might be begun in their national context.<br><br>NPMs recognize whom change implementation will directly or indirectly affect. | |
| (c) NPMs agree how responsibilities for change leadership will be divided between national and local levels, leaving open the possibility of changes over time. | |
| (d) NPMs establish a national level coordinating body (NCB) to provide/coordinate active national leadership.<br><br>Members include representatives of policy makers and all affected groups appointed for five years.<br><br>NPMs arrange professional change leadership training for members. | |
| (f) NCB plans how to publicize the main rationale for/features of change to wider society. *Such awareness-raising to be continued as appropriate throughout the initiation and implementation planning stages.* | |
| (g) NCB convenes national meetings to introduce the change, its rationale and its implications for current practice to representatives from all groups likely to be directly affected. NCB members remain open to responses, suggestions and concerns. | |
| (h) NCB arranges local briefings for local change leaders from institutional leaders upwards, to introduce all aspects of change itself, and the leaders' roles as local planners and supporters of the implementation process. | |
| (i) NCB arranges appropriate professional change leadership training. | |
| (j) NCB prepares a draft plan of the proposed national/local monitoring systems for the change. | |

| | |
|---|---|
| Sends copies to local leaders for comment and to guide their local implementation planning. | |
| | (k) Introduce and discuss the change with teachers in their areas, and identify commonly occurring responses, suggestions and concerns. |
| | (l) Introduce and discuss the change with local teacher trainers, highlighting issues raised by teachers at (k). Assess trainers' existing capacity to meet teachers' training needs. Report back to NCB. |
| (m) NCB considers trainer capacity reports from local areas. Arranges trainer-training as necessary, using expert nationals as far as possible. If national trainer-training capacity not available, consider use of international expertise. *If no access to expertise possible, reconsider change goals in light of teacher-training capacity that is available. Go back to (g).* | |
| (n) NCB coordinates pre-implementation trainer-training. Works with trainers to agree on/arrange implementation training for at least some trainers to develop mentoring and facilitation skills for their future roles as facilitators of ongoing teacher-support processes. | |
| | (o) Work (possibly with leaders from other adjoining areas) to draft local plans for implementation. Plans to cover: support provision for teachers pre-implementation; support provision for teachers during implementation; systems to enable monitoring of implementation in each institution. Local awareness-raising. |

| | |
|---|---|
| | (p) Discuss plans with local institutional leaders, teacher trainers and teachers and adjust in the light of their responses. |
| | (q) Manage/coordinate local pre-implementation teacher training. |
| (r) NCB meets local leaders' representatives for final discussions of what experience so far suggests about the form of change that it is feasible to implement in most schools and agree final adjustments. | |
| | (s) Adjust local implementation plans if necessary. |
| (t) NCB sets date for implementation to begin, in consultation with local leaders and teacher trainers. | |
| Recognizes that contextual differences mean not all areas/schools ready to same degree. | |

**IMPLEMENTATION BEGINS**

| | |
|---|---|
| (u) NCB keeps a close check on monitoring and communications systems during early months to ensure that experiences of implementation from schools in all parts of the country are being collected and commonly occurring problems are being recognized. | (u) Keep a close eye on local monitoring and communications systems to ensure that experiences of implementation from schools in all parts of the area are being collected, and that commonly occurring problems are recognized and made the focus of ongoing local teacher-support sessions. |
| (v) After six to twelve months of implementation, NCB meets local leaders' representatives to consider:<br><br>experiences of implementation so far;<br>whether these merit serious adjustments to the national change aims or hoped-for outcomes;<br>whether there need to be further national initiatives to support the implementation process.<br><br>*Such meetings to continue annually (or more frequently) for at least the first two or three years.* | (v) After six months of implementation, meet representatives of all local groups involved to consider:<br><br>experiences of implementation so far;<br>whether these merit serious adjustments to local implementation plans;<br>whether they need any further local support for implementation process.<br><br>*Such meetings to continue at least every six months for at least the first two or three years.* |
| (w) NCB and local leaders continue to actively lead local implementation towards achieving national-change goals. | |

What does this approach show? The letters below relate to the letters next to each stage above.

**(a)** The above approach takes a long-term view. I mention ten years as a time scale. This would of course need to be considered in the circumstances, but the important point I am trying to make is the need to remove educational change policy from the short-term thinking that seems to afflict much politically motivated national decision making (see chapter 2.3).

**(a–d)** The approach remains initially top down. I believe that for the foreseeable future this will continue to be the case for all national educational-change initiatives. However, in any context, the original national policy makers are unlikely to be able to remain personally concerned with the leadership and management of an educational change initiative over the length of the implementation time span.

**(d onwards)** Leadership and management of the detailed initiation and implementation planning is therefore delegated as soon as possible to a national coordinating body (NCB), which contains representatives of policy makers and all other affected groups (local educational administrators, institutional leaders, teacher trainers, teachers and possibly even the public representing parents). In the light of what I have said (see chapters 2.1 and 3.3), encouraging this broader involvement at such an early stage would in itself represent a big culture change for most national policy-making systems.

NCB remains responsible for national planning of the change for the agreed time scale at (a) and for delegating responsibility for the detailed management and implementation of the local-change process to local leaders as soon as appropriate to ensure that local realties are considered (see chapter 3.1).

**(f)** NCB recognize the need to raise awareness of change in society at large.

**(k onwards)** Local leaders are encouraged to plan with their existing local contexts in mind. (Examples of how this might be done are provided in section 3.) Throughout the initiation and implementation planning process there is ongoing communication between the NCB and local leadership, and there is real recognition that details of the proposed change may need to be adjusted in the light of local realities.

**(d) and (i)** The complexity of change leadership is recognized (see chapters 3.2. and 3.3) and so change leadership training of NCB members and local change leaders is considered.

**(l) and (m)** The critical role of teacher trainers is acknowledged and their training too is part of the initiation stage. It is important to note that if trainer-training cannot be provided, it will almost certainly be necessary to revisit the change aims.

(q–u) The need for teachers to be supported both before the implementation begins and during its early stags is recognized and systems are established to enable such support (see chapter 3.2).

(u) Change implementation only begins when everyone is more or less adequately prepared. This suggests an initiation process that may itself take several years.

(u and v) Once implementation is under way, there is close monitoring at local level. Good communication between local implementers and NCB ensures that NCB has a fairly accurate picture of how the implementation process is progressing nationwide. Any adjustments that may need to be made can be based on evidence of experience.

It can of course be argued that the approach suggested above is too rational and makes far too many assumptions. It assumes that policy makers have a genuine desire to 'reculture' the education system, rather than a desire for short-term political advantage. It assumes substantial funding, consistent trust, good will and enthusiasm from all participants at all levels, and consistent leadership at both 'top' and 'bottom' levels over time. It also assumes a national and/or international environment that is stable enough over time to allow the change process to be worked through. I know that none of these desirable states can necessarily be assumed, and that therefore table 1 represents an ideal. Nonetheless, I believe that the management and leadership of complex-change initiatives will need to begin to incorporate locally appropriate versions of many of the ideas that Table 4.1 proposes, if their success rate is ever to increase.

This section of the book has introduced some important issues that influence any educational-change process and tried to show how they might be incorporated into an approach to change initiation that makes successful initial-change implementation more likely. Section 2 examines three real-life examples of educational-change initiatives in the light of these issues, and tries to show their effects on the change processes and on the people working within them.

# References

## Works cited

Berend, I. (2007), 'Social shock in transforming Central and Eastern Europe'. *Communist and Post Communist Studies*, 40/3, 269–80.

Bereiter, C. and Scarmadalia, M. (1998), 'Beyond Bloom's taxonomy: rethinking knowledge for the knowledge age', in A. Hargreaves (ed.), *International Handbook of Educational Change*, 675–92. Dordrecht: Kluwer.

Blackler, F. and Shinmin, S. (1984), *Applying Psychology in Organisations*. London: Methuen.

Caldwell, B.J. (2004), 'Do current efforts to initiate top down changes fail to support the moral purpose of education?' *Journal of Educational Change*, 5/4, 423–27.

Claxton, G. (1989), *Being a Teacher: A Positive Approach to Change and Stress*. London: Cassell.

Chin, R. and Benne, K. (1970), 'General strategies for effecting changes in human systems', in W. Bennis, K. Benne, and. R. Chin (eds), *The Planning of Change*. London: Holt Reinhart and Wilson.

Cox, C and Lemaitre, M.J. (1999), 'Market and state principles of reform in Chilean education: policies and results', in G. Perry and D. Leipziger (eds), *Chile: Recent policy lessons and emerging challenges*. Washington: World Bank Institute of Development Studies.

Elmore, P. (1995), 'Getting to scale with good educational practice', Harvard *Educational Review*, 66/1, 1–26.

Farias, M. (2000), 'Coping with change: a Chilean case'. Paper presented at the XXVI FAAPI Annual Congress. Comodoro Rivadavia, Argentina.

Fullan, M.G. (2001), *The New Meaning of Educational Change* (third edition). London. Cassell.

Fullan, M.G. (2007), *The New Meaning of Educational Change* (fourth edition). New York: Teachers College Press.

Goodson, I. (2001), 'Social histories of educational change', *Journal of Educational Change*, 2/1, 45–63.

Goodson, I. (2003), *Professional Knowledge, Professional Lives: Studies in Education and Change*. Maidenhead & Philadelphia: Open University Press.

Hargreaves, A., Lieberman, A., Fullan, M. and Hopkins, D. (eds) (1998), *International Handbook of Educational Change*. Kluwer. Dordrecht.

Harvey, S.P. (1999), 'The impact of coaching in South African primary science', *International Journal of Educational Development*, 19/3, 191–205.

Hofstede, G. (1994), *Cultures and Organisations*. London: HarperCollins.

Holliday, A. (2001), 'Achieving cultural continuity in curriculum innovation', in D.R Hall and A. Hewings (eds.), *Innovation in English Language Teaching*, 169–78. London: Routledge.

Hunter, W.J. and Benson, G.D. (1997), 'Arrows in time: the misapplication of chaos theory to Education', *Journal of Curriculum Studies*, 29/1, 87–100.

Joyce, B. and Showers, B. (1988), *Student Achievement through Staff Development*. New York: Longman.

Malderez, A. and Bodoczky, C. (1999), *Mentor Courses*. Cambridge: Cambridge University Press..

Malderez, A. and Wedell, M. (2007), *Teaching Teachers: Processes and Practices*. London: Continuum.

Polyzoi, E., Fullan, M.G. and Anchan, A.P. (2003), *Change Forces in Post-Communist Eastern Europe: Education in Transition*. London: Routledge Falmer.

Riley, K. (2003), 'As national policy makers seek to find solutions to national educational issues, do international comparisons such as TIMMS and PISA create a wider understanding or do they serve to promote the orthodoxies of international agencies?', *Journal of Educational Change*, 4/3, 419–25.

Sakui, K. (2004), 'Wearing two pairs of shoes: language teaching in Japan', *English Language Teaching Journal*, 58/2, 155–63.

Senge, P., Kleiner, A., Roberts, C., Ross, R. and Roth, G. (1999), 'The dance of change: the challenges to sustaining momentum in learning organisations', in *Learning Organizations*. P. Senge, A. Kleiner, C. Roberts, R. Ross, G. Roth and B. Smith, New York: Doubleday.

Wedell, M. (2000), 'Managing educational change in a turbulent environment: the ELTSUP project in Hungary 1991–1998', unpublished PhD thesis. University of Glamorgan.

Young, R. and Lee, S. (1984), 'EFL curriculum reform and teachers' attitudes', in P. Larson, E. Judd, and D. Messerschmidt, (eds), *On TESOL*, 84, 183 –93.

Zeng, Y.H. (2005), Unpublished MA assignment. University of Leeds.

## Further reading

Most of those currently writing about educational change come from the English-speaking world. Most of their examples therefore come from this world. English-language teaching, because of its international reach, is one of the few areas to have looked in any detail at how educational change has been and is being experienced in a genuinely wide range of international contexts. I provide information about possible further readings from this field of study after the case studies at the end of section 2.

### *Journals*

The specialist journal in the area is the *Journal of Educational Change*, which, according to its website

> investigates how men and women, older and younger teachers, students, parents, and others experience change. It also examines the social, economic, cultural, and political forces driving educational change. While presenting the positive aspects of change, the journal raises many challenging questions about educational change as well.

This is the only journal I know concerned entirely with discussions of educational change, across the whole area from strategy/policy to human experience.

Other journals that I have found useful because they sometimes include articles relevant to various aspects of educational change include:

- *School Leadership and Management*
- *International Journal of Educational Development*
- *Communist and Post Communist Studies*
- *Journal of Curriculum Studies*
- *Asia Pacific Journal of Teacher Education*
- *European Journal of Teacher Education*
- *Journal of Innovation in Education*
- *Journal of Organisational Change Management*
- *System*
- *English Language Teaching Journal*
- *TESOL Quarterly*
- *Teaching and Teacher Education*
- *Teachers and Teaching: Theory and Practice*

*Specific reading on the nature of educational change, its complexity and approaches to its leadership and management*

One of the most prolific and influential writers in the area of educational change is Michael Fullan from Ontario Institute for Studies in Education (OISE) in Toronto, Canada. The most recent (fourth) edition of *The New Meaning of Educational Change* (NMEC) is a comprehensive and very readable introduction to the range of issues that any educational change initiative needs to consider. It is full of examples of such initiatives. Almost all come from the North American, UK or Australia–New Zealand context, and so implicitly assume a baseline that cannot be taken for granted in many parts of the world.

Other publications that he has written or co-written include:

Polyzoi et al., *Change Forces in Post-Communist Eastern Europe: Education in Transition.*

This investigates and analyses educational and cultural transitions in the post-communist countries of eastern and central Europe.  Examples in this book represent educational change processes taking place in settings that are very different from those in NMEC and they provide a good sense of what 'reculturing' can mean for all those affected when a previously highly centralized education system suddenly begins to expect autonomous behaviour at all levels.

Fullan, M.G. (2001), *Leading in a Culture of Change.* San Francisco: Josey Bass.

This discusses in detail the range of understandings and skills that educational change leadership requires.

Fullan, M.G. (1993), *Change Forces 1993.* London: Falmer.
Fullan, M.G. (1999), *Change Forces the Sequel.* London: Falmer.
Fullan, M.G. *Change Forces with a Vengeance.* London: Routledge-Falmer.

This trilogy of short books stress the reality that the nature of educational change is non-linear and often seemingly chaotic, and discuss what can and cannot be done in such circumstances, in terms of, for example, policy making and leadership training, to try to achieve real sustainable reform.

*The International Handbook of Educational Change* has now been made available as four separate paperback books, each of which contains a range of articles dealing in detail with a particular aspect of educational change.

Lieberman, A. (ed.) (2005), *The Roots of Educational Change.* New York: Springer.

This looks at the growth of educational change as a field of study and at how ideas about the nature of educational change, and how it can best be approached, have developed over the past 60 years.

Hopkins, D. (2005) (ed.), *The Practice and Theory of School Improvement.* New York: Springer.

The articles in this volume try to develop a theory of school improvement. They look at case studies of school-improvement initiatives in Europe, North America and Australia and consider some of the issues and tensions that arise when trying to 'improve'.

Fullan, M.G. (ed.) (2005), *Fundamental Change*. New York: Springer.

Writers in this volume consider some of the national and international forces that motivate educational-change initiatives. They provide examples of large-scale change initiatives in countries like the UK, Japan and Russia and discuss what the implementation of such changes imply for the professional development of those involved.

Hargreaves A. (ed.) (2005), *Extending Educational Change*. New York: Springer.

This looks beyond educational change itself to external factors that may influence and be influenced by it. Articles for example discuss how change may affect the different groups of people whom it involves and the organizations within which it takes place, and how these may need to adjust in order to be able to be supportive of educational change.

Markee, N. (1997), *Managing Curricular Innovation*. Cambridge: Cambridge University Press.

This is situated in the language-teaching setting. It gives a good summary of some of the approaches to/strategies that have been suggested for the management of educational change initiatives.

Stevens, R.J. (2004), 'Why do educational innovations come and go? What do we know? What can we do?', *Teaching and Teacher Education*, 20, 389–96.

Why is there so much change in education and how can teachers, trainers and administrators work to reduce or slow down the stream of innovations that American schools are subjected to?

Leithwood, K., Jantzi, D., Earl, L., Watson, N., Levin, B. and Fullan, M. (2004), 'Strategic leadership for large scale reform: the case of England's national literacy and numeracy strategy', *School Leadership and Management*, 24/1, 57–79.

This paper takes a very large-scale recent educational-change initiative, considers how in such a setting leadership roles were distributed between local and national levels, and discusses the strengths and weaknesses of the approach that was taken.

## *People and change*

As mentioned in section 1, until very recently far too little notice has been taken of how the people affected by change have experienced educational-change processes. The papers below all relate to educational change in the Anglophone world. Examples from elsewhere will be given at the end of section 2.

Leithwood. K, Jantzi. D and Mascall, B. (2002), 'A framework for research on large-scale reform', *Journal of Educational Change*, 3, 7–33.

This article looks at the processes involved in evaluating large-scale educational reform. It discusses the 'levers' that policy makers try to use to support change implementation and looks in some detail at the human and organizational factors that seem to lead to differences in how those affected respond to change at different institutions.

Hargreaves, A. (2000), 'The four ages of professionalism and professional learning', *Teachers and Teaching: Theory and Practice*, 6/2, 151–82.

Hargreaves discusses how perceptions of what teachers have needed to know and be able to do have changed over the past 50 years or so, and some of the contextual features that have influenced changes.

Hargreaves, A. (2005), 'Educational change takes ages: life, career and generational factors in teachers; emotional responses to educational change', *Teaching and Teacher Education*, 21, 967–83.

As the title suggests this article looks at data from 50 Canadian teachers of different ages and at different stages of their careers, and analyses how they respond emotionally to educational change.

Rust, F. and Meyers, E. (2006), 'The dark side of the moon: a critical look at teachers' knowledge construction in collaborative settings. The bright side: teacher research in the context of educational reform and policy making', *Teachers and Teaching: Theory and Practice*, 12/1, 69–86.

This is an interesting article looking at how teachers' networks in the USA have tried to use the outcomes of classroom enquiry/research to influence policy making. Through doing so teachers have both become more confident about engaging with policy makers and gained a greater understanding of policy.

Pennington, M. (1995), 'The teacher change cycle', *TESOL Quarterly*, 29/4, 705–31.
Guskey, T.R. (2002), 'Professional development and teacher change', *Teachers and Teaching: Theory and Practice*, 8/3, 381–91.

Both present models that try to show the stages that teachers pass through as they engage with change over time.

Oplatka, E. (2005), 'Imposed school change and women teacher's self renewal: a new insight on successful implementation', *School Leadership and Management*, 25/2, 171–90.

This is a fairly rare example of a paper that reports on data from teachers who have experienced educational change as professionally and personally positive.

Section 2:

# Case Studies

# Introduction

Section 1 introduced and discussed some of the most important human and contextual issues that need to be considered by policy makers and planners at the educational-change planning-initiation and implementation stages. I feel these are particularly important if a 'complex' change requiring some degree of 'reculturing' is ever to begin to become embedded in most classrooms, and so eventually become a new part of everyday reality.

Some issues that I suggested policy makers needed to consider at the initiation/planning stage of a complex educational change were:

- what the people who will be affected by the implementation of the change currently think and how they behave
- what adjustment to current norms implementation of the proposed change will therefore require
- how the rationale for the change can be most clearly and appropriately communicated to the different groups it will affect
- how to include representatives of as many affected groups as possible in discussions about realistic timescales for, and contextually appropriate forms of, implementation
- what support of what kinds over what timescale will be needed by different groups of change participants
- how to allocate responsibilities for leading and monitoring change most effectively, and so how to allocate implementation funding
- whether the change will affect other aspects of the education system (e.g. a curriculum change requiring new materials and forms of assessment) and how any such effects will impact on the planning and implementation sequence

To be able to plan bearing these issues in mind, policy makers would in most cases ideally spend time and money on some sort of formal, systematic 'baseline study' to give them a clear picture of where the change is starting from to guide their decision making. When, as is usually the case, there is political and/or economic pressure to move quickly to demonstrate visible evidence of actual implementation, this often does not happen. However, as I hope to show in section 3, I believe that even when time is short there are a small number of questions that, if asked and answered honestly (even if quickly), can provide valuable 'baseline' information to support the change planning process.

Although national policy makers, especially those operating in very top-down and hierarchical organizational cultures, still frequently behave as if change implementation occurs in a neatly rational or linear manner, this is not the case. How could it be when so many people are involved? Instead, as an ongoing process that needs to be sensitive to contextual and human differences, the exact route and speed of change implementation over the years of the process will vary across a country, region or even a group of superficially similar schools in a local area. Issues that I think will particularly influence the speed with which, and degree to which, implementation is likely to occur in a particular local context include:

(a) How fully local leaders understand both the specific change itself and the nature of the educational-change process more broadly, and so both wish and are able to appropriately plan, monitor and support implementation over time.

(b) How carefully the implementation process tries to identify and consider local educational realities. Such realities may include material resources, classroom conditions and the attitudes and ways of behaving that are most common in local educational and organizational cultures. How teachers, learners, school leaders, administrators and parents think, and how this affects their behaviour, will strongly affect their response to, and enthusiasm for, change, and so affect the route followed by the implementation process and its ultimate outcomes.

(c) How much appropriate information and support is provided to help all the above groups understand and/or become able to begin implementing, the 'what' and the 'how' of the change.

Figure 4.3 at the end of section 1 was an attempt to relate some of the large number of possible educational-change variables to each other. However, inter-relationships between the categories and the importance of particular variables for successful educational-change implementation are dynamic rather than static and will alter according to what type of change is being implemented where, and the stage of the process that has been reached.

In this section I present three case studies of educational-change initiatives in which I have been more or less directly involved. They all relate to changes to one or more aspects of language-education provision in state-sector systems. I believe however, that they illustrate aspects of the educational-change process that are widely relevant to those responsible for initiation and/or planning implementation of national and local changes right across the curriculum.

The purpose of this section of the book is to try to connect the decontextualized discussion in section 1 to people's real-life, lived experience. The chapters consider how the educational changes introduced by each case were planned and implemented. They also highlight some consequences of initial planning for later implementation. Each case could, if examined in detail, fill a complete book. It is therefore important to point out that what follows represents a summary, and so a simplification, of each case.

Each chapter begins with a background section in which I situate the case in terms of the change it was trying to achieve and why the change had been perceived to be necessary. I then discuss aspects of the manner in which it was initiated/planned and implemented, relating the discussion to the main issues of leadership, understanding of the existing context and availability of communication and support systems presented at (a) to (c) above. The final part of each chapter considers what the case can tell us about issues/variables that seemed to make a real difference to the change process in a real situation.

# Chapter 5

# A sudden need for English teachers

## 5.1 Background to the change

This change initiative was part of a larger process similar to the one outlined in situation 1 in the introduction to this book. As part of a major national political reorientation in the country, a decision was made to move from a very centralized education system where 'in every school every teacher taught children the same content from the same textbooks on the same day' (Horvath 1990: 209), to a much more devolved system. Universities became autonomous and local governments became responsible for the administration of schools. The interpretation of the curriculum and choice of materials was devolved to individual schools, and within these, decisions about exactly what happened in classrooms was the responsibility of the teachers of different subjects. This massive decentralization of the education system was soon followed by a new National Curriculum, whose suggested teaching approaches, teacher–learner behaviour and hoped-for outcomes represented a clear shift from a more transmission-based towards a more interpretation-based educational culture (see Figure 3.2 on page 39).

The decentralization of education was just one part of wider national (and international) political changes that the country was undergoing. These led to a sudden surge in the demand from parents for their children to be taught English. There was a need to train large numbers of new English teachers. The Ministry of Education (MoE), in collaboration with a foreign governmental agency, made a plan to respond to this demand through the establishment of eight new English-language teacher-training institutions situated across the country. The visible educational change that was proposed was that students at these institutions should study English as a single major (all other university programmes were double majors), and should be able to graduate as English teachers with a university degree that qualified them to teach at all levels of the state system after three years' study rather than the five years that was customary under the existing regulations. The explicit aim of the initiative was thus to increase the number of English teachers in schools.

The decision was made to situate these new three-year programme (3YP) English teacher-training institutions within, but independent of (in terms of funding and curriculum) existing universities and teacher training colleges across the country. Although each 3YP shared the same aim, each was situated within a different local context. In the discussion that follows I sometimes refer to the 3YP change process as a whole, and sometimes to the planning and implementation process in one particular 3YP institution, which I refer to as 'the case study' below. The 3YP initiative as originally conceived lasted for approximately six years, albeit in different forms at different institutions. Thereafter, different 3YP institutions, to the extent that they survived at all, developed completely differently.

## 5.2 The change-initiation/planning stage

### 5.2.1 Change leadership, timescale and funding

A formal agreement was signed between the MoE and the partner agency for a period of three years (exactly the length of one proposed three-year course). The initial capital costs of setting up and equipping the new institutions and the ongoing funding of student places and staff salaries were met by the Ministry. The partner-agency funding paid principally for the costs for expatriate 'experts', the provision of professional support for 3YP staff and relevant professional materials and resources, for example libraries, for the 3YP institutions.

Given that the political complexion of MoE and, in the context, their senior civil servants, changed three times during the seven to eight years of the initiative's life time, the lack of consistent Ministry guidance over the case-study period is not surprising. However, in fact all active MoE leadership and management support and guidance ended at the initiation stage, almost as soon as the broad aims outline, physical structure and funding mechanisms of the 3YPs had been agreed. It was unclear whether anybody in the Ministry had even short- to medium-term responsibility for planning, monitoring or evaluating the content or outcomes of the programme. There was no guidance regarding what 'type' of English teacher it was hoped the 3YP would produce. There was no communication between the policy makers and the implementers about the aims and/or duration of the 3YP initiatives. Newly recruited 3YP staff at the case-study institution thus wrongly

> took it for granted that it was going to be a long term thing. There was no indication as to sustainability or that the financial support might be finite. (Wedell 2000: 87)

MoE's lack of guidance as regards 3YP content and outcomes meant that decisions about these were strongly influenced by the external partner.

Although all 3YP institutions were established at the same time for the same purpose, there was little uniformity from the start. Staff members at the HE institutions with which they were associated viewed their 'arrival' with very varying degrees of enthusiasm and comprehension. This, together with the differences in institutional structure and culture between colleges and universities and the regional differences between the various parts of the country, meant that from the very beginning each 3YP institution differed to some extent in its degree of genuine financial and curricular autonomy, its size, the background and attitudes of its staff, and its physical setting.

At the case study 3YP, leaders of the existing English faculty at the host university from the very beginning viewed the additional premises, facilities and staff that the 3YP funding enabled, as resources that would one day probably revert to the faculty. They chose one of their longest-serving colleagues as director of the 3YP to ensure that departmental priorities were not forgotten. This hidden institutional agenda was never communicated to new 3YP staff, who joined what they thought would be a long-term, independent and innovative teacher-education institution.

The timescales to which the national policy makers committed themselves were short. There had been no obvious consultation or discussion with anyone regarding what the new 3YP institutions were supposed to do or how they were supposed to do it. The time available to identify 3YP institution leaders and for them to find and equip premises, recruit staff and students, and work out and prepare what and how to teach the students, was in most cases less than six months.

> QUESTION TO CONSIDER
> In our case study 3YP, the director was a regionally well-known English-grammar expert. He had no experience of teacher training or of ultimate responsibility for leading an institution. If you were in his position, what concerns would you have?

Section 1 suggested the critical role of local-change leaders. I think the new director would have had many concerns. Due to his lack of teacher-education expertise, he would be likely to be uncertain about:

- what and how the institution was supposed to teach the trainees once they arrived
- what teaching and learning materials needed to be bought or designed
- how to equip the building for teaching teachers
- how to advertise the programme to students in the recruitment literature, since there were no stated aims for the 3YP
- whether staff, facilities, a syllabus and teaching materials would be ready by the time the students arrived

Due to his lack of prior leadership and management experience, he might also worry about the new roles that he would need to play as director in terms of, for example:

- leading and managing new staff who were themselves not experienced teacher trainers
- developing a strategic plan for the design and implementation of a teacher-education curriculum whose content and expected outcomes are very different from those of the curriculum with which he is familiar

## 5.2.2 Understanding the wider and local-change context

As you may sense from what I have said so far, there was political pressure on the part of both MoE and their foreign partner to start the programmes very quickly. The time available for assessment of the existing social, educational and organizational environment was very limited, and serious consideration of how these might influence what would be appropriate content and teacher-training approaches for the 3YP did not therefore take place. As a senior local participant said, 'all the mistakes that were committed later were due to the fact that I had to do everything very quickly' (Wedell 2000: 82).

The people likely to be more or less directly affected by the new teacher-training institutions included their future staff, and trainee teachers, and the leaders, teachers, pupils and parents at the schools where the trainees would do teaching practise and possibly eventually work. I also include the members of the existing English departments at the 'host' institutions, who might view the establishment of the 3YPs with some concern, as direct competitors for a limited pool of students.

---

QUESTION TO CONSIDER

Policy makers had not defined the teaching content and approach for the three-year programme (3YP) in any way.

If you had been responsible for leading the implementation process and designing the 3YP English teacher-training curriculum, what information would you have wanted about the wider and immediate context? Why?

---

I would have wanted to find answers to at least some of the following questions:

1. Should each 3YP expect to help and be helped by the others?
2. Can 3YPs expect to get support from their 'host' English departments?
3. Will it be easy to recruit trainees, and will they want to become teachers when they graduate?
4. How does society currently view education? What do they expect it to be like? What do they expect teachers to know and do? What about learners, what do they expect English teachers to know and to be able to do? How involved are parents in their children's education? How are teachers evaluated? Is the local area typical?
5. What are the aims of learning English at school according to the new English curriculum? What do the important exams test?
6. How do schools and university departments work as organizations? Who makes the final decisions? Is everybody encouraged to contribute? Do staff usually share ideas and cooperate? How do people usually communicate with each other? Is information freely available?

I would have wanted to find out something about each above area, because they could potentially affect:

- the degree of uniformity that it will be possible to achieve among 3YP programmes and the speed with which they can be established (1 and 2)
- how easy or difficult it is likely to be to recruit students and so how we should set about doing so (3)
- what kind of a training programme we will need to try to design; the programme content and approach we will need to consider if graduates are to be more or less prepared for the educational reality in which they will be expected to work (4–6)

I look at each of the above questions and what issues their answers raise for the wider 3YP context and/or the case study below.

1. The eight 3YP programmes were associated with universities and colleges all over the country. Universities considered themselves superior to teacher-training colleges, and even among institutional equals there was little tradition of inter-institutional cooperation. Different regions of the country had different histories and were united only in their dislike of the capital. The eastern part of the country had always been poorer than other regions and so was at least slightly resentful of the south and the west.
*So spontaneous collaboration was unlikely, yet collaboration was desirable. What could be done to foster cooperation? Whose responsibility was it to do so?*

2. There was little enthusiasm for change in the case study's host university according to a member of the 3YP staff:

> There wasn't a felt need; they only had things to lose. ... I think in terms of ideology they were completely resistant. I'm sure they would have said, 'We're happy with the model we've got. We'll develop it ourselves if we think there is a need for it.' (Wedell 2000: 89)

This was acknowledged by one of the university English-faculty leaders:

> I can imagine that somebody from the outside will say that we didn't want to change either in the beginning. (Ibid: 100)

The 3YP was in direct competition with the existing 'teacher training' provided by the host institutions. In addition, generous funding was initially provided for the establishment of all 3YP institutions, and this was funding that might otherwise have gone to the host institutions. Salaries for 3YP staff were set slightly higher than those for existing academics in the host institutions, even though most of these new staff had little or no teacher-training experience.
*In such circumstances, what support could 3YPs expect from their host institutions?*

3. Nationally teachers' salaries were poor. In a society where status was increasingly related to wealth, their status was low. However, the ability to use English was a scarce and therefore marketable commodity. Consequently it would probably be quite easy to recruit students, but many of those who graduated from the 3YP

might not want to become teachers. There were many other career opportunities open to them that paid better.

*How would the scarcity of English skills in the wider society affect the extent to which 3YPs would be able to achieve their aim of supplying the state sector with sufficient English teachers?*

4. Society viewed education as the transmission of fact-based knowledge from teachers to learners, to be memorized and later tested. A case study 3YP staff member saw it thus:

> You need education to get more knowledge. When you have learned facts you have knowledge. You go to school to learn facts and when you have learned them you gain knowledge. (Ibid: 113)

Most people (parents) were less interested in education than the product of education, the certificates and the degrees that could lead to good jobs. Success in examinations was therefore seen as extremely important and frequent testing was a feature of schools at all levels. Classrooms were traditionally hierarchical. The teacher was in charge, learners were expected to be silent and listen to the teacher lecturing. The concept of knowledge as fact meant that any question had a right answer. Teachers were therefore expected to know the answer to any question that the learners might pose and were worried by questions that they could not answer.

English teachers who were trained in the existing system were expected to have a high level of linguistic proficiency and to thoroughly understand the facts needed to to teach grammar and word formation rules. They were also expected to know facts about English literature, culture and history. The educational part of their training was also almost entirely academic, spending virtually no time on the development of practical teaching skills. Teaching practice in schools involved 10–15 hours of teaching, supervised by teachers who had no specific training for their role. Teaching, like all other 'subjects', was seen as objectively assessable and evaluated by performance in an 'exam lesson'. A member of the 3YP staff who was a graduate of such a programme commented:

> We started our careers without having any guidance as far as teaching is concerned. I had to struggle for 3 or 4 years until I knew how to teach. I knew about Pestalozzi and teaching in China 2000 years ago but nothing about real teaching. (Ibid:121)

*How would the 3YPs want to adjust the content and process of their new programmes?*

5. Within society at large the product of education was emphasized, and the main aim of learning English was to pass the high-stakes exams. These exams continued to test mostly facts about the language rather than the ability to use it.

*Would it be necessary to bear the need for trainees to be able to help their learners to pass such exams in mind when designing the new programme?*

6. The way in which the host university heard about the case study 3YP initiative was as follows:

I heard about the whole plan from ... who was the Dean who received some message from the Ministry. The task was clear, that a new type of teacher training had to be established. The Dean had to solve this problem. (Ibid: 101)

This top-down approach was typical of the organizational culture within education more generally. The hierarchy was stable and clear. At each level of the hierarchy people were expected to carry out decisions handed down from higher up. Everyone was used to being told what he or she should do. As the quote from Horvath above suggests, before the decentralization most teachers at all levels of education had little need for, and little experience of, planning or taking autonomous decisions.

Communication of information within organizations was on a need to know basis and teachers at all levels were expected to carry out their jobs without asking questions. Such a culture was not conducive to active cooperation and collaboration among teachers, whose role (see 4) was to know their subject and be able to answer any questions about it, and who therefore were potentially always a little afraid of judgement and possible criticism.

*The 3YP staff came from an educational and organizational culture that had only expected teachers to react. What support would they need to develop the skills/confidence needed to proactively take the many academic, practical and strategic initiatives needed?*

As mentioned previously, no baseline study that might have identified contextual issues such as these was carried out at the planning stage. National policy makers gave no guidance regarding programme content and approach. They provided no leadership or management support. At the beginning of the implementation stage leaders of 3YP institutions and their staff had only their own previous experience on which to base their attempt to establish the 'new type of teacher training'.

### 5.2.3 Clarity of expectations and provision of support

The 3YP programme was a collaboration between national policy makers (MoE) and a foreign partner. MoE planners were members of a new and inexperienced government, and detailed knowledge of the region among most representatives of the foreign partner was largely confined to knowledge of the capital. The main aim of the initiative, to produce more English teachers quickly, was quite clear. There was however no coherent agreement about what the nature of the training should be.

Given this lack of clarity, the very top-down organizational cultures at the time (see 6 in 5.2.2 above), and the lack of a common language, communication between MoE and the foreign partner, and between them and the host institutions, was often poor. As a result, (it later became clear that) there were different understandings of what had actually been agreed. This revealed itself in terms of lack of clarity about who, at what level of the hierarchy, was ultimately responsible for deciding what, and in disagreements about the degree of financial and curricular independence that the 3YPs should have from their host institutions.

The lack of guidance from national policy makers about what form the 3YP was supposed to take, and the limited prior experience of national 3YP staff, meant that the expatriate staff recruited by the foreign partner as deputy directors of the various 3YP programmes took a significant leadership role. They became responsible for planning the content and approach of the 3YP curriculum, even though they had little or no in-depth understanding of the organizational or educational cultures in which they would be operating.

The first 3YP institution was established in the capital one year before all the others. Given the lack of any other guidance, the model that they established had great influence as an important point of reference and starting point for 3YPs at all other institutions. To a significant extent the model adopted here became, in various adapted forms, *the* 3YP model, the new model of teacher education that separated 3YP programmes from those that already existed and that linked 3YP staff at different institutions.

The director of this first institution was the most prominent English-language teaching professional in the country, and with his foreign deputy the model took the form of a much more practical training, intended to be closely linked to the reality of teaching in schools. It had less focus than was traditional on literature and linguistics, instead emphasizing methodology and language competence. It made a conscious choice to base its curriculum around an outcome for teacher education that was beginning to become current in Anglo-American language teaching circles, that of a 'reflective' teacher. Such a view of the outcome of teacher training implies a curriculum that enables trainees to experience and recognize that professional development is an ongoing process, and that they remain responsible for continuing to develop their professional understanding and skills through thinking about and acting on the explicit and implicit outcomes and experiences of their classroom teaching, throughout their professional lives.

Retrospectively, the choice of this aim seems a little incongruous, given that in the country from which the foreign 'experts' came, the aim of teacher education was moving in the opposite direction towards preparing teachers to be good 'technicists' (Malderez and Wedell 2007: 13) able to teach a predetermined national curriculum in a consistent manner. This is a good example of how, as a result of political changes, and the ideological changes that often accompany them, educational policy makers in different countries may, at the same point in time, introduce changes that move their education systems in opposite directions along the continuum introduced at the start of section 1.

---

QUESTION TO CONSIDER
Does such a 'reflective' model 'fit' the existing concept of education and the teacher's role as discussed in 4.2.2?

---

Some ways in which I think the idea of a reflective teacher in the sense expressed above might conflict with the existing concepts include:

- the idea of a reflective teacher suggests that there is more to good teaching than the successful transmission of facts to learners, since if good teaching only involved this, a teacher who knew the facts thoroughly would have completed his/her professional development
- if learning to teach is an ongoing process and involves more than the transmission of facts, then it is possible that there will often be more than one possible answer to the many questions that may arise in the classroom. If this is so then the definition of a 'good' teacher needs to be altered to include the ability to help learners deal with and choose among multiple points of view
- if there are often potentially multiple points of view, it is possible that learners may sometimes know better than their teacher. It also raises questions about whether assessment that is purely based on the accurate recall of facts can in fact be considered to accurately represent what learners know
- all of the above have implications for the roles of teachers and learners in the classroom, and for how these roles are perceived by interested parties in the wider society

### 5.2.4 Conclusion

The initiation stage of this educational change initiative was hurried and carried out without any real consideration of the context into which the 3YPs were being introduced. The national policy makers withdrew from active involvement as soon as the infrastructure – in terms of funding and agreements with host institutions – had been established. They took no part in deciding what form this new training should take. They did not consider whether the social climate was one in which the 3YP graduates would wish to become teachers, and so whether the purpose of the whole initiative would be supported. Responsibility for planning, monitoring and supporting 3YP implementation was effectively passed to the expatriate employees of the foreign partner with whom they had agreed to collaborate. These knew little about the context for which they were planning. I next discuss how, given the above, 3YP programmes began to be implemented.

## 5.3 The change-implementation stage

### 5.3.1 Matching change to local realities

Little attempt had been made to investigate contextual issues at the change initiation stage. Each 3YP institution thus had to cope with the wider environment in which it found itself as best it could at the implementation stage. This was made more difficult by the other changes taking place in both national and local environments throughout the implementation process.

The 3YP was initiated in response to a sudden surge in demand for English teaching at schools, which itself was a result of wider political and economic changes in society. Attitudes nationally and locally had been very open to and positive about these wider changes at the point that the 3YPs were established. However, as the reality of what they implied for people's daily lives became clearer, enthusiasm for the whole idea of change lessened. There was growing unemployment and inflation rose to well over 20 per cent a year. While some people were becoming rich, more felt poorer. More families had two working parents, leading to a perception among those working within the education system that there was less parental supervision of children and that learners behaved less obediently at school.

New patterns of relationships between local and central government under the new decentralized system were still developing. Local educational administrators were grappling with responsibilities for which they had no training. Regional economic differences meant that local authorities in different parts of the country increasingly varied in the funding they devoted to schools. Parents' contributions to school budgets began to become important. With education being seen ever more instrumentally as a means to the achievement of material goals, parents who contributed to school funds began to demand a say in how schools were run. In such an unusually unstable wider environment, deciding which local realities represented 'reality' (and so should be the benchmark for decisions about how to approach the implementation process) were difficult to assess, even if anybody had thought of trying to do so.

There were however also certain environmental constants throughout the implementation period. One was the poor pay and therefore ever-lessening status of teachers. Three years after her graduation, the daughter of the case study 3YP director earned five times as much as he did after decades as a university teacher. Comments from 3YP students and staff show perceptions at the time:

> I don't think today being a teacher is recognised at any level. It's more like you pity somebody who's a teacher. (Ibid. 168)

> It is almost impossible for a young person with a family to make ends meet on the ridiculous salary they get at Primary or Secondary school. (Ibid. 169)

Teachers' poor pay had several negative consequences for the 3YP initiative. It soon became clear that fewer and fewer graduates of the programme wished to become teachers. This was very demotivating for 3YP staff.

> I think it is quite harmful the knowledge that you know that the students you have are not going to be teachers. So there is no real meaningful aim for them in terms of spending their time here. So the validity of the whole thing is gone. (Ibid. 224)

Inflation meant that by the second or third year of implementation, 3YP staff salaries were insufficient to enable them to work full time in their 3YP role. This of course affected their ability to work as team, making it very difficult to arrange meetings to coordinate teaching, and so ultimately diminished the coherence of the 3YP programme that was offered.

Another constant feature of the national, and therefore all local, environments was the largely unchanged educational culture in most schools. There had been huge legislative changes in national education policy. A new national curriculum was introduced, emphasizing the need to develop learners' skills as well as teach them facts. Schools were legally entitled to decide how to interpret the curriculum through syllabuses that were appropriate for their learners. However, this was a further example of 'paper' changes alone being insufficient to lead to actual changes in what happened in classrooms. The lack of central government support and guidance meant few schools accepted the opportunity to change. The teaching and learning of English (and other subjects) continued to be seen by many teachers, head teachers, educational administrators and especially parents as the transmission and memorization of whatever knowledge about the subject was contained in the prescribed textbook for the year of study. The format and content of high-stakes tests, unchanged despite the above policy shifts, strongly supported this perception.

As a result, the methodological training that trainees on every 3YP received, which emphasized the practices, techniques and activities that were then thought to be helpful for providing learners with both knowledge about the language and the ability to use it, was not always implementable in schools when trainees went out on their teaching practice. 3YP trainees themselves were of course also 'products' of the existing educational culture. Some of them therefore found it difficult to take the oral-language-development classes that were central to the first year of the programme as seriously as the as 'real' learning that was done in linguistics or literature classes. The pupils in the schools in which they practised were no different, as some case-study trainees reported:

> The only thing they [Primary school pupils] have to learn is grammar, because that is what is to be asked in the entrance exams for the grammar schools. I know it doesn't come from the kids but their parents. (Ibid. 171)

> I have a student who is always trying to write down everything I'm saying. I go 'don't write everything down'. He comes to me after class and asks, 'how shall I prepare for you?' I say 'try to cooperate, you don't need to write everything down'. There are some students like him. They have to change their whole point of view about learning. (Ibid. 171)

The 3YP model of language teacher training (which everywhere was some version of that described at 5.2.3 above) was not consistent with the reality prevailing in the majority of schools.

Nonetheless, newly recruited staff in the eight 3YP institutions had to design and implement a curriculum for their trainees. I next discuss the extent to which they were supported in developing the new skills that their work on the 3YP demanded.

## 5.3.2 Support for learning the 'what' and the 'how' of change

The backgrounds of staff recruited to provide the 3YP training varied from one institution to another. In the case study 3YP they were all graduates from the host university English department who had become successful secondary-school English teachers. They had no background in teacher training.

Since they had previously been teachers, staff from the host university viewed their 'promotion' to teacher trainer with scepticism. Throughout the first years of the implementation process, university staff openly made negative comments about the academic quality of the curriculum and the academic ability of both 3YP staff and students. This lack of support from the established university staff had the positive effect of making 3YP staff more determined to develop their own independent programme, but also meant that in most institutions staff felt undervalued and unsupported by their immediate academic environment. This feeling was strengthened in the case study setting by a sense that the 3YP director lacked the necessary leadership qualities (see 5.3.3). It was not until the third year of implementation, when teachers and school leaders in practice schools evaluated trainees' professional knowledge and skills positively, that staff in the case study 3YP began to receive any positive responses to their efforts.

National policy makers made no suggestions regarding the content of the new 3YP curriculum. The model adopted by the first institution to be established therefore provided important guidance. However, the material and human resources available in the capital were not necessarily available everywhere else and so their model needed to be reinterpreted by each 3YP institution to become useable.

The 3YP implementers everywhere were also working in a constantly changing policy environment (see 5.3.3). They had little opportunity to consolidate their development of one set of understandings and skills before a new set were needed. Implementation at the case-study institution showed the truth of the statement that 'We never know what implementation is or should look like until people in particular situations attempt to spell it out through use' (Fullan 1991: 92). The process took the form of continuous cycles of larger- and smaller-scale planning and implementation to meet immediate needs for syllabuses and materials, followed by re-planning and re-implementation in the light of feedback from trainees and eventually schools, and in response to unpredicted policy changes. I believe that for any complex change that entails 'reculturing' of some kind, even if implementation has been planned with the local context in mind, the process at local/institutional level will always involve such a series of planning, trying out and re-planning cycles before any final form implementation can be reached.

As I am sure you can imagine from the above description of their background, staff of the case study 3YP had a huge amount to learn and to do. They had been recruited only a few months before the students arrived. They had only the 'reflective' 3YP model discussed earlier to guide them, but few clear syllabuses or materials to begin teaching with. Their previous experience was of being teachers in the educational culture outlined at point 4 in 5.2.2 above.

QUESTION TO CONSIDER
What help would you hope to receive in their situation?

Some help that I would have needed would have included help to understand:

- the implications of a reflective model of teacher education for the content of the 3YP, and how it needed to be adjusted to 'fit' the local context. What sorts of courses needed to be offered? In what order? What weighting should be given to each course in the whole programme?
- how to develop syllabuses, and choose or design materials to support their teaching
- and become able to use teaching approaches that were consistent with the ideas about teaching and teacher development that a local version of reflective model espoused
- how to assess trainees' knowledge and skills
- how to build relationships with schools. After all trainees were supposed to spend most of their third year in schools. Which schools? What preparations would need to be made in order to ensure that the school supervisors understood what the 3YP programme was trying to achieve?

3YP staff had to learn a lot very fast if they were to be able to offer their trainees a coherent teacher-training programme. MoE had made no provision for supporting such learning and responsibility for doing so therefore fell to the foreign partner, and the expatriate deputy directors whom they employed, and who of course arrived with their own assumptions about what was appropriate deriving from their prior experiences and their very different educational culture.

The first support provided for most new 3YP staff immediately before the first group of trainees arrived was a one-month course in English-language teaching methodology. This was a well-established and internationally recognized course, based on beliefs about the nature of language, learning and language-teaching methodology regarded as appropriate for training teachers to work in *private* language schools rather than in *state*-education systems. Given their brevity, such courses have little choice but to promote a particular 'communicative' language teaching method to be followed, rather than a flexible teaching approach based on a set of principles and techniques that need to be adapted to local circumstances. Negative feedback from early trainees on the over-zealous application of this 'communicative method' in the early implementation stage at the case study 3YP, added to the constant adjustments to teaching content and methodology that were required throughout the first years of the programme.

However, the 3YP was not merely a language course and each 3YP institution had to develop a curriculum, syllabuses and materials in order to be able to implement the teacher-training aspect of the programme. To begin with, responsibility for doing so was largely devolved to the expatriate deputy directors. In the case study institution, the new staff members were encouraged to participate as fully as they were able in this process (see 4.3.3), and the foreign agency recognized the critical need for them to be professionally enabled to participate.

The next phase of formal support, provided throughout the first few years of the implementation process, therefore consisted of short (one week or less) professional-development workshops led by expatriate 'experts' for 3YP staff from all eight institutions. These focused on discrete areas of professional expertise such as testing and assessment, syllabus design and dissertation supervision. 'Experts' lack of understanding of participants' prior experience meant that these sometimes assumed too much prior knowledge and so increased implementers' anxiety. Overall, though, these played an important role in establishing a 3YP identity by providing a forum where implementers could meet colleagues from other institutions and share their ideas, problems and insecurities in a supportive environment. The following quote from one member of the case-study staff gives a sense of this:

> There was this kind of solidarity because these places (3YP institutions) were looked down on by their main departments so there was a kind of national solidarity and the people we got to know we treated each other like colleagues. There wasn't the sort of envy ... we were willing to cooperate. (Ibid. 219)

Given how much there was to learn, and the rush to learn it in order to be able to teach the hundreds of trainees who had been recruited, it is not surprising that the emphasis in the above workshops, and of the less formal support provided by deputy directors within 3YP institutions should be on 'how to do things' rather than on the theoretical rationale for doing them in a particular manner. Consequently, it was not unusual during the first years of implementation for 3YP implementers to know 'what to do' without necessarily being able to explain 'why'. This added to their overall stress during the implementation period.

A final stage of professional support provided by the foreign agency was to fund implementers to attend specialist professional international summer schools and one-year professional MA programmes overseas or in-country through distance learning, to follow up areas introduced at in-country workshops. Overseas MA degrees were not recognized as a qualification in the national context, and so on paper did little to enhance the perceived expertise of those who gained them. However, in the case study setting, 3YP staff who did successfully complete such courses were unofficially acknowledged to have reached a higher level of professional competence by the host university leadership. This recognition was to have important implications for their future employment prospects when the 3YP ended (see 5.3.3).

A further, very important, more indirect, form of support for the implementation of the 3YP, provided at all institutions to a varying degree, was the professional development provided for the in-school supervisors of 3YP trainees' teaching practice. One of the most significant 3YP innovations was the extension of teaching practice from the handful of hours on the existing university programmes to six months or even a full academic year. For such an extended teaching practice to make sense, it was essential that there should be reasonable consistency between the professional messages that trainees received on the 3YP and those they received from their in-school supervisors when they arrived in schools. Consequently, an additional feature of the implementation process at most 3YP institutions involved the recruitment of a large number of school supervisors and the development and teaching of a training programme that would enable them to support trainees as fully as possible during the teaching practice. As with all other aspects of implementation, the development of appropriate programmes was an ongoing process, with the balance between methodological and supervisory/mentoring training changing over time. (For more information on this aspect of the change process see Medgyes and Malderez 1996.)

The implementation process thus involved 3YP staff with a huge professional challenge. Over several years they were exposed to a mixture of formal professional development support and actually having to 'do' all sorts of new things within the 3YP implementation setting, a mixture of what Schon (1983) would call 'received' and 'experiential' knowledge. Not all staff had equal opportunities to receive formal support, since opportunities were affected by unstable foreign-agency funding, which often had to be spent within certain time limits, and declined substantially over time. However at the case-study institution, by the time the 3YP ended (see 5.3.3), many implementers felt that they did have the professional competence and confidence needed to implement 3YP programmes. As some of them stated:

> We were not in a position to have more ownership over the programme in the beginning. I think we are at a stage where we can take over.

> At the beginning there was this immediate need, this pressure. There was actually a staff here who hadn't got the knowledge they needed to have and at the same time they had to act on it. Now we have it.

> We have reached autonomy and independence. There are quite a few very experienced and highly developed people in the profession. (Ibid. 225)

I would be very happy to report that the 3YP story ended here with, in the case study setting at least, a general feeling of satisfaction at staff having been reasonably well supported through a fairly successful implementation process. However, as the next section shows, changes in the wider environment meant that in the case-study setting as soon as one set of challenges had been more or less successfully met, another appeared that required a whole new process of professional change. This new stage of the change process, coming at a point when national policy makers' interest in the 3YP had entirely withered away, and when the foreign partner's commitment was rapidly diminishing, was far less well supported.

### 5.3.3 Leadership of the 3YP change process

In 5.3.1 I pointed out that the national environment was itself constantly changing throughout the implementation process. Within the education system, decentralization meant that the role of institutional leader became far more complex than it had been when the system was more top down and centralized, and when leading at a local level was therefore principally a matter of ensuring that instructions from higher-ups were followed. This era of multiple changes was confusing for administrative and institutional leaders at all levels.

As authority was taken away there was no experience or competence to cope with the newly gained freedom. Frustration cried out for a paternalistic state. (Horvath 1990: 212)

The ultimate leaders, the national policy makers, did not themselves have the experience to offer effective support or guidance to either local-education leaders or to the very much less significant 3YP initiative. Instead, their policies made the 3YP implementation process ever more complex.

Policy makers had introduced a new national curriculum. Local education administrators and school leaders were left to try to cope with the leadership demands of their newfound responsibilities for education in their areas and/or the implementation of the new national curriculum in their schools, largely unsupported. It is not surprising that in the circumstances many opted to stick to what was familiar and in many schools teachers continued to be expected to complete the allocated textbook by the end of the term or year and stick to teaching the facts needed for success in exams. Where this was the case, even if school supervisors were broadly sympathetic, 3YP students on teaching practice found a mismatch between what they had been trained to do and what they were expected to do in real classrooms. The content of, and approach to, 3YP methodological training had to be frequently readjusted to reach a workable compromise between ideals and realities.

National leaders undermined the 3YP initiative more dramatically through new legislation. The whole purpose of the initiative had been to train large numbers of English teachers to meet the demand for English throughout the school system. Prior to the initiative, only graduates of the five-year university training had been entitled to teach at upper-secondary level. Teachers for other levels were trained at four-year colleges. Since 3YP graduates were to be able to teach across the system, it was assumed that the qualification they would receive would be equivalent to a five-year university degree. This made the 3YP an extremely attractive option, and enabled the initiative to recruit many able trainees. However, even before the first group of trainees had graduated from the case study 3YP institution, a new Higher Education Law was passed stating that 3YP graduates, while still being able to work across the system, would receive a college-level degree. They could if they wished spend two more years at university to get a 'proper' degree. At the same time the passing of a new Public Service Law formalizing the grading and salaries of all public servants highlighted the significant difference in salary and status between those with university and college degrees.

> QUESTION TO CONSIDER
> What effects would you expect this downgrading of the 3YP qualification to have on 3YP trainees, their teachers and future recruitment?

Some of the effects that it did have at the 3YP case study institution were:

- the academic level of the students applying to join the 3YP became lower. This meant that staff had to make further adjustments to course content and teaching that had originally been designed for trainees of a higher level
- programme graduates became even less likely to actually enter teaching since their salaries, as teachers, which were already low, would be even lower than expected. More of them sought jobs outside teaching or went to the university for two more years
- the 3YP staff became more and more aware that very few of those whom they were training were actually interested in going into teaching. This was of course demotivating for them, especially given the hard work that they had put in, and were continuing to put in, to becoming competent and confident teacher trainers

National-level leadership, therefore, rather than being supportive, consciously or unconsciously undermined the implementation of the 3YP initiative that it had introduced.

Local leadership varied greatly from one 3YP context to another. In the case-study context the director brought little relevant prior experience to the role. His previous role as deputy dean of the university English faculty in the days before university autonomy had not prepared him at all for the twin roles of leading the professional development of a new teacher-training institution and developing an institutional identity and strategic plan.

While there was no formal allocation of responsibilities between the two, professional leadership of the implementation process was largely delegated to the expatriate deputy director. She was professionally extremely competent but had little experience of the educational and organizational culture of the environment and consequently found it difficult to understand the need to make some of the adjustments that were essential if a broadly 'reflective' teacher-training curriculum was to work in the local context. She had an inclusive leadership style that encouraged staff to be as involved as they felt able to be in the mass of syllabus and materials design and development work that characterized the first years of implementation. She recognized that interaction, collaboration and mutual aid were critical contributors to professional learning and established the tradition of weekly meetings at which everyone could discuss all issues. She therefore encouraged the introduction of a very different organizational culture to that existing in the schools at which most staff had previously worked, one characterized by trust and collaborative teamwork, which staff reacted to very positively: 'We were all for it, we loved it, that's why we did it' (ibid. 211).

As implementation progressed, 3YP staff and student numbers increased, as did the amount of new work needing to be done just to keep abreast of the syllabus and teaching demands of the three years of the programme. The intimacy and constant teamwork of the early stages lessened, and these factors together with the deputy director's lack of willingness to adjust ideals to local realities led to confrontations. Staff turned to the director. Due partly to personality, and partly to the fuzziness surrounding roles and responsibilities, he was unable to mediate effectively. In the organizational culture in which staff had spent most of their working lives, leaders were expected to lead. His inability to make clear decisions when staff had disagreements with the expatriate deputy therefore severely compromised his authority. After the first two years the deputy left and was replaced. For the following five years the staff remained stable. While the intensity of the teamwork and collaboration that had characterized the early stages did not return, the tradition of regular meetings, open communication and access to information for all remained a feature of the 3YP culture, recognized by staff:

> We were absolutely encouraged to participate and it was absolutely necessary for us all to participate in everything. Never when anybody had an idea were they discouraged or shut up by anybody higher up. It often happened that ideas were passed on and nothing happened, but nobody's participation was ever discouraged. (Ibid. 216–217)

In this sense the case study 3YP institution (and some others) did develop its own identity and sub-culture, very different from that existing in the host-university English department, and most other educational institutions at the time.

While the teacher-training professionalism of the case-study institution clearly grew throughout the implementation stage and, as noted above, reached a point where external support was no longer perceived to be necessary, the development of decision-making and strategic-planning skills was far slower. The previous top-down culture had been so pervasive that neither the director nor any of the 3YP staff had any experience of institutional strategic planning. As the director said, 'the most difficult of this is planning curriculum-wise, to be able to see what I have to do say in two years time' (ibid: 179). Most aspects of forward planning for the 3YP while it continued, and for the next phase of the change (see below), therefore remained the responsibility of the expatriate deputy director for as long as the post existed.

The 3YP staff's lack of involvement in strategic decision making throughout the implementation stage, meant that most of them were also not centrally involved in planning how to respond to the end of the 3YP. National policy makers, first through their policy decisions above and later through stating that they would no longer fund students to study on 3YPs, clearly saw no future for the institutions as they existed. What then was to become of the physical infrastructure and the staff? Again, in the case-study context, it was the foreign partner who strongly influenced the decision that was made.

Just prior to the publication of the new Higher Education Act downgrading the 3YP qualification, the foreign partner commissioned an external evaluation of the 3YP in the eight institutions. This, when made public soon after the above Act, pointed out that the quantitative aims of the initiative were not being met, since relatively few trainees saw teaching as a desirable career. It recommended that the 3YP initiative should cease to be a separate set of institutions with a separate teacher-education curriculum, and should instead begin to try and merge with, and so influence the curriculum of, the existing five-year university/four year college systems. It further suggested that continued funding from the foreign partner and continued provision of expatriate staff should be made contingent on there being evidence of this merging process occurring.

In the foreign partner's eyes, the outcomes by which the success of the implementation initiative would be judged thus changed. Initially they had been quantitative: the number of qualified (the term had remained undefined) teachers trained and entering the school system. This had been at best partly successful. The outcomes now became qualitative: the extent to which innovations in English teacher training introduced by the 3YP curriculum could be seen, in some form or another, in the longstanding existing university/college teacher-training programmes.

The national 3YP initiative finally petered out when MoE announced that it would no longer fund 3YP students. Some 3YP institutions ceased to exist. The 3YP in the capital was supported by the foreign partner in setting up the country's first PhD programme in Language Pedagogy in collaboration with its host university, and the 3YP itself continued quasi-independently there for a few more years.

In the case-study setting, after protracted negotiations between the 3YP leaders and the university English faculty, the faculty's long-term strategy of eventually absorbing the 3YP bore fruit. The staff and premises of the 3YP became a new department within the faculty responsible for all teacher training. Some of the 3YP innovations were accepted, with faculty leaders acknowledging their superiority.

> I think the greatest achievement of the new programme has been to demonstrate how important teacher training is, how much you need in terms of the number of methodology classes and the amount of time devoted to teaching practice. (Ibid. 236)

> The methodology component is better (on the 3YP) towering above what we have here. Your model is ideal here too. Nobody questions that. (Ibid. 237)

In addition to its teacher-training responsibilities, the new department would offer an Applied Linguistics academic track to undergraduates and a distance upgrading programme for English teachers who did not have a full university degree. A minority of 3YP staff, those without M-level qualifications, were regarded as insufficiently qualified to be university teachers and lost their jobs. Those that remained faced the beginning of a new implementation stage, involving new personal and professional changes. First they had to register for, and within five years obtain, a PhD to be regarded as qualified to be university teachers. Next they had to restart the process of designing a new programme, this time with the emphasis on more theoretically grounded academic Applied Linguistic courses. They had to learn about how to design a distance-learning programme and the text and online materials to support such learning. They had completed almost a decade of constant change and were now entering a second.

## 5.4 What does the case study tell us about educational change?

What I have written here is a very condensed account of some features of an educational-change initiative that spanned almost a decade. It was a complex change (Fullan 1992) involving the reculturing of the change implementers in terms of their beliefs about the content and process of language-teacher education and the development of new practical skills to enable them to provide appropriate initial teacher training for English teachers. It involved perhaps a hundred staff and several thousand students. In terms of its scale it was therefore quite small. Nonetheless, I feel that it reinforces certain messages about educational changes that are very relevant to those who lead it.

### 5.4.1 Legislating for change does not mean it happens

If policy makers genuinely wish to introduce new teaching and learning practices that will lead to new learning outcomes for most learners in most classrooms, they need to understand that legislating for a change is merely the beginning of a long change planning and implementation process. Every stage of the process will be made more difficult for all involved, and the human and material resources expended will be less likely to yield the hoped-for outcomes, if policy makers do not take the trouble to think carefully about:

(a) the reasons for their legislation and how these can best be communicated to those who will be affected
(b) which features of the existing context may support or undermine the change that they hope to bring about, and try to act to minimize the influence of potentially undermining features of the context (such as in this case the pay and status of teachers, and the mismatch between curriculum aims and high stakes assessment)
(c) what extent of reculturing the change represents, and what this implies for the provision of adequate support over time to enable implementers and everyone else who will be affected to learn how to behave in a different manner

Policy makers cannot, as was the case here, merely sign the enabling legislation and detach themselves entirely from the detailed change planning and implementation process, and still expect change to occur.

### 5.4.2 Complex educational change takes time

This has a number of consequences.

First, in the current rapidly changing global environment it is unlikely that all features of the wider national or even international environment in which a change was initially planned will remain the same throughout the change-implementation process. For example, implementers in the case study, who were intensively exposed to change on a daily basis, reported that it took them 3–5 years to feel mastery (Fullan 1993) of the teaching behaviours and practices that the 3YP introduced and of the principles on which they were based. Only then could they be effective disseminators who could persuasively influence others. While this developmental process was going on within individual implementers, aspects of the original wider environment in which the change was planned were themselves changing in ways that were more or less conducive to the achievement of the hoped-for change outcomes. One example of such a change from the 3YP is the national growth of alternative job opportunities for those with good English skills during the implementation period, which made it less likely that 3YP graduates would wish to enter teaching. Depending on the nature and extent of such changes in the external environment, the actual outcome of implementation may be more or less similar to what was originally planned.

If this is so, then national policy makers need to:

- try to be realistic about the timescale of their proposed changes. If they are planning long term, it is possible that some aspects of the environment that they take for granted as they carry out their initial change planning may have changed by the time the implementation process is well under way.
- recognize that, consequently, for complex change initiatives, the plans that they make at the beginning of the change process will almost certainly need to be adjusted over time if they are to continue to be able guide the implementation process.
- accept that a change process is never a purely rational, linear chain of context neutral events in which certain inputs will 'deliver' certain outputs. Any such process will need to be evolutionary, in the sense of adjusting its route and even its aims according to what is happening in the wider environment.
- monitor the wider external socio-economic and political environment for changes that are likely to affect the rate or route of implementation.
- respond to any such changes by adjusting expectations accordingly.

A second consequence of the long-term nature of much complex educational change is that during its extended implementation process the institutional (school or local educational administrator's office) change environment may itself change as a result of participating in the implementation. This case study showed institutional change implementation process to be a series of incremental planning and implementation cycles. The second and subsequent cycles were based on the experience of implementing previous cycles. If there is fairly stable staffing and a consistent effort to continue implementation, then as cycle follows cycle the context in which planning or implementation occurs becomes different from the context that existed when the implementation process began. From one cycle to the next, some or all of those involved now have experience and understanding of the new practices that they did not have previously, which they can use to participate more fully and/or help others to do so during next implementation cycle.

If this is so, wherever possible it would be wise for national policy makers to:

- try to maximize the stability of any ministry or other national-level personnel that they make responsible for the ongoing support and/or monitoring and/or evaluation of the change-implementation process. This can be a major problem in political contexts in which a change of minister or of government also means a change of all senior civil servants.

Similarly, local planners need to:

- recognize the importance of maintaining stable staffing among those leading and implementing educational changes within all affected local administrative and educational institutions.

A final consequence of the long timescales involved relates to the experiences of the implementers. Throughout the many planning-implementation cycles out-lined above, case-study implementers invested a great deal of personal effort in becoming more confident practitioners. Maintaining the necessary levels of effort can be very tiring and stressful. High levels of initial enthusiasm can make it possible for implementation to begin. However, even if implementers are sup-ported in becoming more professionally confident over time, their enthusiasm for continuing to make the effort to become as adept at, and confident about, the new change practices is likely to diminish after a while. This will certainly be the case if too much change is expected too quickly, if there is insufficient time for con-solidation of new skills, or if the 'hygiene factors' (Carey and Dabor 1995) of the job, the salary, working conditions and interpersonal relationships are not per-ceived as satisfactory.

3YP implementers *in the case-study institution* faced constant demands for pro-fessional change throughout the implementation stage, as it gradually became clearer how the imported 'reflective teacher' model of the curriculum needed to be adjusted to meet local expectations. There was little explicit acknowledgement of the efforts they were making by leaders at any level. There was no point at which they could relax and feel they had reached a point at which they felt comfortable with their professional expertise without further changes being expected of them. There was no chance to stop for a while. As the implementation process pro-gressed, the value of their initially adequate salary was whittled away by inflation and they had to find other work, which they had to fit around their very demanding primary job. The lack of obvious appreciation of their efforts, together with the accumulated stress and tiredness, diminished enthusiasm for change considerably, as one staff member made clear:

> I think people here at the start were very enthusiastic, saving the world. Now it's broken to smithereens. We've ended up a bunch of disillusioned people. Now professionalism appears but enthusiasm is gone. (Ibid. 223)

If change implementers are to continue to actively implement, both national policy makers and local-change leaders need to consider how they can:

- balance periods of active change planning and implementation with periods

during which implementers have time to consolidate what has already been achieved
- make sure that where genuine effort is being demanded from implementers over time, they feel that their efforts are appreciated both by overt encouragement and by close attention to the above 'hygiene factors'

### 5.4.3 Successful change requires genuine devolution

I have frequently mentioned policy makers' tendency to see educational change as merely a matter of expecting or requiring teachers to carry out what has been legislated for on paper in a uniform manner and at uniform speed across the country. Policy makers in strongly hierarchical, top-down, organizational cultures such as the one illustrated in the case study are likely to find it hard to conceive of educational change as an open, variable and unpredictable process, whose outcomes can rarely be predicted in any detail.

However, even in organizational cultures that claim to be genuinely more decentralized, national policy makers still tend to expect educational change implementation to be a uniform process. By emphasizing the expectation of universal predictable outcomes, they make it difficult for local-level change leaders to genuinely consider local realities. This makes it more likely that successful large-scale change will remain as elusive as ever.

### 5.4.4 Use of 'off the shelf' models

It is frequently the case that national change leaders who are themselves not clear about how to implement a change that they wish to introduce are tempted to turn to imported models that appear to offer instant solutions. In the above case it was not actually the policy makers who imported the model that informed the development of the 3YP curriculum, since they entirely ignored the question of how the change was to be implemented.

The responsibility for choosing a model on which to base implementation planning was thus taken by the institutional leadership of the first 3YP in the capital. Overall, their willingness to actually make a decision was probably a blessing since it provided a starting point for implementation planning in all provincial 3YP institutions. However, one effect of importing a teacher-education model developed for use in one cultural setting (the capital) into other cultural settings (the 3YP case study and other 3 YP settings) was to make the implementation process more complex in many such settings, since implementers had to discover which aspects could, and which could not, be made to 'fit' the expectations of the existing educational environment through trial and error.

If policy makers wish to use an imported model to support their understanding of the educational change they wish to implement, they need to:

- have a clear idea of what they hope that the proposed changes will achieve

- be clear that the claimed outcomes of any 'off the shelf model' that they intend to use do actually substantially overlap with what they want to achieve
- be clear about the main cultural norms and material conditions presupposed by the imported model
- carry out a baseline study of the current 'cultures' of their society, their education system and those who work in it, and of the conditions that are normal in affected classrooms
- understand which features of the model are more or less likely to be acceptable to/fit the material conditions of the current system
- emphasize those features that are likely to be less difficult for people to accept/operationalize in the initial stages of the implementation process, and think about the extent to which the other features may be introduced later

### 5.4.5 Successful experience of change makes continuation more likely

An actual example of a successful change initiative can be a powerful aid to convincing those who are resistant to, or sceptical of, the value of a proposed change. The fact that a noticeable proportion of the 3YP case-study trainees going into schools received good feedback from supervising teachers and school leaders, made it more difficult for the previously sceptical leaders of the university English faculty to ignore the ideas emanating from the 3YP, and the skills of 3YP staff who understood how these ideas could be incorporated into a teacher-training curriculum.

The lived experience of the implementation process, the perception of which aspects of change do or do not work in the context, and do or do not add benefit to the existing way of doing things, will influence what aspects of change 'continue', in the sense of eventually becoming existing norms of an education system or some of the institutions within it. Such perceptions of benefit may be both professional and purely pragmatic. In the 3YP case-study environment, therefore, the English faculty took decisions about which aspects of the programme to incorporate into the existing five-year programme on both grounds. For example, devolving responsibility for the teacher-training component of the course to the 3YP staff represented both an acknowledgement of their greater skill and understanding of this aspect of their professional responsibilities, and relief that few faculty staff would now have to be responsible for something that they had never been keen to engage in, namely teacher training.

### 5.4.6 The value of collaboration and mutual aid

Some of the 3YP case-study staff's most positive memories of the implementation process relate to the opportunities that existed for them to meet colleagues from other 3YP institutions who were working to try to implement the same change aims. They found such meetings valuable both personally and professionally.

Personally they valued the opportunity to make ongoing contact with others with whom they could discuss their worries and uncertainty, and professionally it was useful to hear about and learn from how other institutions were approaching the solution of the many implementation challenges.

This suggests that policy makers should plan implementation in a manner that:

- recognizes the value of supporting implementers through enabling regular structured opportunities for them to meet, discuss and learn from each other.

## 5.4.7 Trained teachers are only *part* of any successful educational-change process

Good teacher training is one key aspect of enabling change to reach the classroom. However, while change cannot reach classrooms without 'qualified teachers', other factors also influence what happens in classrooms. If either the prevailing educational culture or other components of the subject area (especially high-stakes exams) are not in harmony with the teaching–learning principles underpinning the change, then even if teachers have been well trained, it is almost certain that many of the hoped-for positive effects of such training will fail to appear in the majority of classrooms. Policy makers thus need to remember that:

- the multiple variables that determine the nature of any education system are interdependent. One variable cannot usually be changed without at least thinking about how the change will affect its 'fit' with the others

# Chapter 6

# A change in teaching approach

## 6.1 The background to the change

In chapter 1 I introduced some common reasons why policy makers might decide that an educational change is needed. One increasingly common reason is a perception that an existing education system that emphasizes the transmission of a body of learned knowledge to all learners is no longer adequate to enable them to develop the skills they will need for life and employment in a rapidly globalizing world. This case study looks at one aspect of an educational change that was introduced for this reason.

As part of a wider national educational-change planning process involving the development of new curricula covering all subjects, policy makers decided that the approach used for the teaching of English in secondary schools needed to move away from its existing grammar-translation emphasis towards a more 'communicative' teaching approach. This it was hoped would eventually result in learners who not only knew about the language, but could also use the language, and so enter higher education or employment with tangible skills that would be of value both to them personally and to the wider community.

The policy change towards the implementation of new teaching approaches was introduced without a great deal of obvious detailed planning by national policy makers. There was no particular timescale attached to the change. Funding (for the implementation of new approaches in English classrooms) was in the first instance principally focused on providing in-service training for a relatively small proportion (nationally) of 'good' existing teachers. There was no explicit statement as to how such teachers should then be used, but since there were sanctions to ensure that they returned to their original schools after training, there seemed to be an implicit expectation that they would 'cascade' their new understandings and skills down to institutional/local colleagues when they returned. Funding continued to be available for the support of such training for well over ten years. In-service training is the focus of the case in this chapter.

## 6.2 The initiation/planning stage

### 6.2.1 Leadership timescale and funding

The initial change planning did not include any changes to either the national English textbooks used in each school nor the high-stakes English exams that learners took at the end of their secondary-school studies. Neither was there any immediate change in the pre-service teacher-education curriculum.

While central government kept firm control of the education system throughout the change period, responsibility for planning the details of the in-service training process was devolved partly to local-level education administrators/institutional leaders, who were responsible for deciding on which teachers should be allowed to take the exam to compete to be sent for in-service training, and partly to English departments at universities identified as being appropriate providers of such training. As will become clear, neither national policy nor either set of local leaders seem to have felt any responsibility for what happened once the training was completed.

---

QUESTION TO CONSIDER
Can you identify any inconsistencies in the change planning process as described so far?

---

I notice the following:

- the policy makers seem to have ignored the interconnectedness of the different components that influence how any subject is taught. The aim is to change the classroom teaching approach, but no plans have been made to adjust textbooks, exams and initial teacher training to 'fit' the approach. This is likely to negatively affect how the new approach is received if existing materials cannot be used with the approach or it conflicts in any way with success in high-stakes tests.
- there does not seem to be a clear allocation of responsibility for ensuring that leaders in the local environments (or in the university training departments) develop systems that will enable returning teachers to share their new understandings and skills with their colleagues. This may severely limit the extent to which new understandings and skills can be disseminated more widely.

### 6.2.2 Understanding the national and local change context

The existing approach to the teaching of English naturally reflected the main features of the educational and organizational culture of the country. The organizational culture of the existing education system was extremely centralized, top down and hierarchical. Classroom teachers were expected to teach a national curriculum according to strict guidelines regarding what should be taught when. The educational culture had been more or less stable for many years, and had a very clear concept of what knowledge, learning and teaching meant, and of the roles and behaviours that were appropriate for teachers and learners. These existing roles did not encourage autonomous, individual decision-making.

In terms of the perceived purpose of education and of the expected roles of teachers and learners within the classroom, the educational culture was again situated towards the 'transmission' end of Figure 3.1 on page 33. English teachers taught a centralized curriculum using standardized nationally approved textbooks. English classes were based around the detailed study and explanation of the grammatical structures and vocabulary items that appeared in the texts that formed the core of each unit. These in turn represented what was to be learned from each class, the expectation being that new structures or vocabulary items would be memorized by the learners before the next class, during which one or more learners' recall might be tested orally. Much or even most teaching was done using the mother tongue, and use of English was largely restricted to completion of the written grammar or vocabulary practice exercises that followed each text.

The new teaching approach proposed was, as in chapter 5, based on a model of the language learning–teaching process imported from educational cultures that assumed different material classroom conditions and different classroom behaviours from both teachers and learners. While the existing focus was on the memorization of grammatical structures and vocabulary items in order to reproduce these correctly in low and high stakes tests, communicative approaches had very different emphases. Classroom learners were to be exposed to a far wider range of language inputs, in terms of reading and/or listening to texts, and expected to understand and analyse these in far less detail than was traditionally the case. Such texts' purpose was often to serve as introductions to, or stimuli for, oral and written classroom practice activities that would encourage learners to interact with each other and/or the teacher using more or less guided/modelled language for more or less realistic purposes. The explicit teaching of grammar and vocabulary on which the existing method was based, and which provided teachers, learners and parents with a clear measure of what had been learnt in each class, was given less prominence. Instead, the majority of classroom time was to be spent on activities with far less visible outcomes, involving exposing learners to examples of the language being used for more or less real purposes and providing opportunities for them to practise using their knowledge of English to comprehend and express more or less real meanings.

---

QUESTION TO CONSIDER
What might existing English teachers find difficult or challenging about adjusting their teaching to such an approach?

---

Some of the many difficulties/challenges might include the need to:

- move away from the idea that teaching a language principally entails providing learners with correct facts about the forms of the language

- use more English in the classroom, to 'manage' and support the wider range of classroom language-use activities
- move beyond 'lecturing' about the language to develop a more flexible set of teaching behaviours suitable for supporting a wider range of activities
- develop techniques that will encourage learners who are used to listening to the teacher to participate actively in practice activities
- rethink how to assess learners to include some assessment of performance as well as of knowledge
- develop strategies and skills to adapt and adjust existing materials to provide learners with different types of learning activity

English teachers were in short supply nationally. Their salaries were poor and economic changes in the more developed parts of the country meant that proficient English speakers could find alternative, better-paying employment quite easily. While the country had a very centralized education system and a widely shared set of norms underpinning its educational culture, there was considerable economic variation between different regions. Policy makers decided to use the case-study in-service training programme to try and support the professional development of English teachers in less well-developed areas of the country, by giving teachers from such areas priority on the in-service programmes.

Such regions of course also tended to have been less exposed to economic and social changes and therefore to be more conservative in their educational and organizational cultures. The 'reculturing' required of teachers from these areas would thus be greater and need considerable time. There is no evidence that national policy makers encouraged university staff in the more developed areas where the programmes were situated to bear trainees' backgrounds in mind by trying to build elements of 'cultural continuity' (Holliday 2001) into their programmes. Nor did they advise educational leaders in trainees' home regions about how they might prepare to receive and use the trained teachers when they returned.

If teachers from less-developed regions were to be successfully trained in the new approaches, their teacher educators needed to be people who understood and were able to explain and demonstrate use of the new approaches themselves. National policy makers appeared to recognize the need for 'qualified' trainers, since they situated the training programmes at a small number of well-known and prestigious language-teaching universities across the country where understanding of the ideas underlying the new teaching approaches and familiarity with the associated teaching techniques was likely to be greatest.

## 6.2.3 Clarity of expectations

The introduction of a new approach to the teaching of English was part of a wider educational-change policy that aimed to begin to adjust the outcomes of secondary education, in terms of the understanding and skills that learners were equipped with by the time they left school. A new language curriculum did in very general terms present an outline of what was to be expected of learners in terms of language knowledge and skills. However, the lack of detailed guidance and the lack of parallel changes to textbooks and examinations suggests that at the planning stage policy makers had not yet fully identified what the intended outcomes of the change, of which the in-service training was part, should be.

To be eligible to apply for the in-service programmes, secondary teachers needed to have a college-level diploma, at least five years, English teaching experience, and to be working in a school in named, less-developed, regions. To sit for the entrance exam teachers had to be recommended by their institutional heads and/or local-level educational administrators. The programmes lasted for two years, during which trainees continued to be paid their teachers' salaries. If they passed the appropriate final exam (in all universities bar one, an exam specifically written for them) they would obtain a BA degree. The courses were to include a substantial language-development component, courses in the ideas about language and learning underpinning communicative approaches and extensive methodological inputs and practice opportunities

By situating programmes in prestigious universities, policy makers ensured that participants would have kudos when they returned to their local areas. However, no formal plans were made outlining whether, how and to whom their new skills and understandings were to be communicated on their return, what role their in-service training was supposed to play in enabling them to do so effectively, or how the university training departments might contribute to the dissemination process. Expectations of the change were therefore fuzzy in terms of the outcomes of both the larger national change and of the case-study in-service programmes.

### 6.2.4 Conclusion

The planning stage of the case-study change was inconsistent in a number of ways. On the one hand policy makers seemed to recognize certain crucial needs: the need for the training to be long and thorough enough to be able to 'reculture' teachers in the directions that the new approaches entailed, the need for training institutions to have qualified teacher educators, and the need to try to ensure that the benefits of the training provision was weighted towards areas where the need was greatest.

On the other hand planners failed to communicate the rationale for either the national or the specific English language-teaching case-study changes to local educational leaders and the wider society. Nor did they consider the extent to which there would need to be 'reculturing' outside as well as within the classroom if the hoped-for new teaching approaches were to be implemented. They were vague about how the training might be more widely disseminated, and their failure to adjust teaching materials and examinations in parallel with the new approach, almost guaranteed that any wider effects of the training programmes would be diminished. This case therefore represents a further example of policy makers' lack of appreciation of the range of factors that may influence/be influenced by a complex educational change.

## 6.3 The implementation of the change

### 6.3.1 Matching change to local realities

The plans for implementing the case-study change were limited to the provision of the in-service teacher training programmes outlined above. The local realities I will discuss here are therefore those existing in:

- the in-service teacher-training environment
- the working environment to which the teachers returned after their programme

#### 6.3.1.1 The in-service teacher-training environment

The teachers who were successfully admitted to the in-service programmes were from less-developed areas. They were older, less proficient at English and less exposed to modern ideas than most other undergraduate students at the institutions at which they studied. They came from more conservative backgrounds, where the existing teaching and learning norms were most firmly entrenched. They had been chosen to apply for a place on the programme as a result of their perceived excellence as teachers using the existing grammar-translation-focussed method. Their prior experience thus meant that the majority therefore arrived with strong preconceptions about their role as students and very clear expectations of their teachers.

The universities offering the programmes were in developed areas. They had been chosen because their staff were thought to be most likely both to understand the theories underpinning communicative approaches, and how to explain, demonstrate and provide practise in the methodological techniques needed to implement such approaches in classrooms. Language teaching for undergraduates at these universities already showed signs of more communicative approaches. Teachers used English in class for more of the time. Many teachers, while still focusing on explicit teaching of grammar and vocabulary to some extent, had also begun to develop new professional roles as organizers, managers and facilitators of more or less linguistically controlled practice activities. Such teachers expected their students to be far more proactive and participative than was the case in the classrooms in which the trainees had previously been teaching.

> QUESTIONS TO CONSIDER
> How would newly arrived in-service trainees expect to be treated by their teacher trainers?
> How would the university staff expect their new 'students' to behave?
> Can you see any mismatch?

The trainees arrived at the university bringing with them the assumptions about language teaching and about teacher and learner roles that they had developed through their prior teaching-learning experiences. They, as teachers who had been using the traditional grammar-translation method in their classrooms for at least five years and who had been granted the in-service training opportunity as a result of their success in doing so, expected to be taught more or less as they had been teaching. They expected the university teachers to take full charge of what was to be learned in the classroom, and to teach both English and the theories and practices of communicative-teaching approaches in the same manner and with the same detail and thoroughness as they had always taught English in their class-rooms. As learners they expected to be told what to do, to have new language points or professional ideas fully explained, in their mother tongue if necessary, and to receive a clear correct answer to any question they might pose.

The university staff, on the other hand, viewed their responsibilities differently. They were already more familiar with different teaching approaches. Their language teaching materials were different from those that the trainees had been used to using in their school classrooms. For example, the trainees as teachers had been used to explaining small amounts of English reading text in great detail and with great concern for how language forms were used to express meaning. As students they were now presented with far greater quantities, and more varied types, of written and listening texts, which they were expected to process for general meaning, without necessarily having new structures and/or vocabulary explained or being told exactly what they should learn from them.

The two sides were situated at significantly different points along the broadly conceived continuum of educational cultures (see Figure 3.1 on page 33). The differences were so great that both sides felt the other was failing to carry out their teacher or student roles appropriately. As one trainee saw it in the university-learning context:

> ... there is such a kind of vagueness which confuses me, it's like walking in the air. In the past the teacher explained everything to us, the clear grammatical rules, the explanation of vocabulary and simple memorisation made us feel confident and easy. It seemed I had learned all the knowledge the teacher taught us. (Ouyang 2000: 405)

The trainees/students felt that the teachers were not doing their job properly. They were not explaining unknown items in the text, but asking them to infer from context. They were not telling them what the correct answer to each question or the correct outcome to each activity was, suggesting that there could be more than one correct answer or conclusion. They did not give them specific items to memorize and learn and so at the end of a class it was not clear what the purpose of the class had been and what had actually been achieved. The teachers/teacher trainers conversely felt that the students/trainees were unwilling to make decisions for themselves, reluctant to participate in classroom language and/or practise teaching activities, unable to approach problems independently and over-reliant on the guidance of the teacher.

Each side's expectations were therefore initially unfulfilled. However, since the trainees perceived themselves as (and were perceived to be) students in the university setting, it was they who had, over time, to adjust to the teaching approaches and culture of the training environment. Over their two years of study they therefore went through a process of personal and professional reculturing as they developed the confidence to start making teaching and learning decisions for themselves, and the ability to independently analyse and develop solutions to teaching and learning problems that they encountered. As one of them reported:

> Now I have learned to judge, to decide, to act, to do everything I should do as soon as possible and all by myself. And I think if I am facing another great change in my life I will certainly be able to make a more active response. For the training has helped me to form an excellent ability in analysing things and solving problems. I have learned to rely on myself, to make full use of my ability, and to seize any opportunity. (Ouyang 2000: 409)

Most did eventually succeed in graduating successfully after their two years of study. The length of the training was fully vindicated. However, even so, making the transition from being a teacher who had full mastery of the knowledge and professional skills needed to successfully transmit a stable, unchanging, defined body of language knowledge to learners, to a teacher who felt fairly confident about their own language proficiency, about the rationale for their teaching approach and about their professional ability to help learners begin to develop their own language skills, represented a great challenge.

### 6.3.1.2 The trainees' working environment

I have already said that there appeared to be no consideration at the planning stage of what trainees would do when they returned to their schools. Consequently, there had been no attempt to raise awareness of how the trainees might have changed and how such changes might be used for the benefit of education in the local area, among leaders, colleagues, learners or parents in their home environments. In 6.3.1.1 I explained that there was an initial clash between trainee and trainer expectations due to their very different prior experiences. Since those remaining in the trainees' original working environment had had little or no reason to alter any of their beliefs and behaviours while the trainees had been away, the stage was set for a further mismatch of expectations on their return.

---

QUESTIONS TO CONSIDER

How might the graduating teachers returning to their working environment now differ personally and/or professionally from teachers who had remained behind?

How might local leaders, teaching colleagues and learners react to any such differences?

How might returned trainees feel?

---

Most graduating teachers returned to their working environments different in many ways. Personally they had experienced living in a big city in a developed part of the country for two years. They would have had many new experiences, and met a wide range of different people and been exposed to many new ideas. Their view of the possibilities available to them would have been altered to a greater or lesser extent. Professionally they had begun to develop characteristics more similar to those working on the 'interpretation' side of Figure 3.1 (see page 33). They returned as teachers who were more confident in their language proficiency and more able than they had been previously to make decisions about what and how to teach. They were also, to differing degrees, now aware of the need for, and able to manage and organize the provision of, an English classroom in which learners had at least some opportunity to interact.

Educational and institutional leaders and colleagues who had remained at home retained the characteristics of the more 'transmission-based' educational culture that had characterized the returning teachers before they left. Insofar as they had thought about what to expect of those excellent teachers whom they had sent for further training, they could only expect them to be as they had been before they left (excellent 'transmission oriented' teachers), only even better after two years spent studying at a prestigious university.

Instead however, many trainees who returned were now teachers who no longer fitted the norms of the working context or indeed the immediate wider society. Some were teachers who now tried to use mostly English to teach English, which some colleagues interpreted as 'showing off' or which learners said they could not understand. Some tried hard to encourage learners to begin to interact in English in the classroom, causing noise and so potential disruption to their colleagues. Many trainees, when they first returned at least, tried to lessen the almost exclusive classroom focus on study of the forms of the language. Without this focus their learners' results in the 'knowledge-based' examinations were no longer so high. Parents were disappointed and questioned the learning value and cultural appropriacy of encouraging their children to spend time using the language in class. School leaders and educational administrators, whose original nomination of the returned teachers had often been based on their ability to obtain good exam results, now faced teachers for whom exam results were no longer necessarily the main criterion of good teaching, and who sometimes made unsolicited suggestions and independent decisions about how to teach. This challenged (albeit in a very minor manner) the existing top-down organizational culture, and so could seem aggressive and threatening to the harmony of the institution. The following quote shows what one teacher experienced on returning to her original school:

> After all we have done ... we were ready to apply our skills ... to our workplace in our hometown. We soon discovered a huge gap between our vision and social reality. Traditional ELT methods ... have prevailed for so many years. We used CLT (communicative language teaching) methodologies and tried our best to make the classroom activities as interactive as possible, but I got negative feedback suggesting that CLT produced students who could 'only speak loud in class but scratch their heads in tests and exams'. It was as difficult as cutting out a path from a pile of rocks (Ibid. 410).

QUESTION TO CONSIDER
How would you expect returning teachers to feel when confronted with such responses?

I think that many of them might have:

- felt confused about what the point of the whole training programme experience had been. Why spend two years studying and learning new skills if nobody appreciates them, and in fact finds them threatening?
- felt resentful/angry that after all the effort they had made during the training to try and make the professional changes that were expected, now nobody is interested
- become reluctant to continue to make much effort to use their under-appreciated new skills and reverted to the status quo
- begun to think about leaving teaching entirely and using their English skills in some other workplace, or leaving teaching in the local environment and going somewhere where their skills would be more valued

Once again the trainees found themselves out of step with the prevailing educational culture, as is simply illustrated in Figure 6.1.

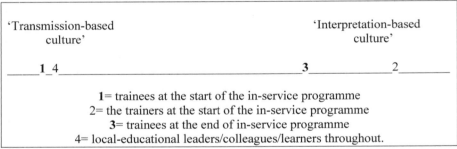

Figure 6.1    Trainee 'fit' with their study and working environments

Exact positions along the continuum are less important than the demonstration of the cultural 'gap' between the trainees and their trainers (at the start of the in-service programme), and the returning teachers and their leaders, colleagues and learners (when they came home). As is clear, this gap was significant throughout. Such a gap and the potential for cultural and personal uncertainty that it engenders is extremely stressful for any implementer. Such stress, compounded by the clear lack of appreciation for their implementation efforts, did little to enable the understandings and skills developed during the change efforts (in line with the national policy change) to influence the returning teachers' institutional or wider local environment.

## 6.3.2 Support for learning the 'what' and 'how' of change

One could argue that those teachers who had the opportunity to attend the in-service programmes were well supported. Despite the universities' lack of sensitivity towards the experiences that trainees arrived with, discussed in 6.3.1.1, the programme length, their own hard work and the generally 'qualified' trainers meant that many did graduate with an understanding of, and an ability to use different approaches to, the teaching and learning English.

However, those who had sent them were not helped to understand either the 'what' or the 'why' of the changes to teaching that new national policies hoped to introduce, nor 'how' trainees might be used to support local implementation of such policy on their return. Similarly, no effort was made to alert the universities to the need for them to work with trainees on contextually appropriate strategies for introducing aspects of the new approaches into schools and classrooms in their local areas in unthreatening ways. Ultimately this lack of concern with wider implementation of the hoped-for change meant that in many local contexts the opportunity to implement what had been learned from the in-service programmes was minimal. The investment in the training thus resulted in the provision of usually only one or two potential change agent(s) within each local county or city district. As we have seen, if they remained in their original workplace, they were likely (initially at least) to be frustrated by their leaders' and colleagues' lack of interest in their new skills and understandings, and so at the lack of effect they were able to have on English teaching in their institutions and/or immediate wider environments. Consequently, many left.

## 6.3.3 Leadership of the change process

As in the previous case study, national policy makers did little to lead the change process after their initial decision to encourage the development of more learner-centred teaching approaches. Given the complexity of the proposed change for the existing educational culture, there was a lack of appropriate leadership at all levels. Lack of preparation for, and clarity about, the dissemination process at the national leadership level inevitably resulted (given the top-down organizational culture) in a lack of clarity and a failure to prepare among leaders at the local level. Consequently, in most local contexts the potential benefits of the investment made in training were underexploited.

Since the case-study programme ended, national policy makers have continued to try to implement the introduction of new approaches to the teaching and learning of English and other school subjects. New national English textbooks, which do reflect the recommended more 'communicative'-language teaching–learning approaches, have been developed and are in use in all schools. Adjustments have also been made to the content and weighting of what is tested in high stakes exams to try to reinforce the message that learners should develop their language skills as well as their language knowledge. These measures, together with the ever-increasing recognition across society that education needs to enable learners to develop new skills if they are to participate fully in the continuing economic and social development, have helped to raise awareness of the value of new English-teaching–learning approaches among local administrators, educational leaders, teachers and parents. Case-study teachers returning to their working environments today would probably have a more welcoming reception.

## 6.4 What does this case tell us about the educational-change process?

The themes that emerge from this case reinforce many ideas that have been discussed previously.

### 6.4.1 Trained teachers are only *part* of any successful educational change process

Complex educational change can require a 'reculturing' process to take place, albeit to differing degrees among the different groups affected by the change. In this case, while unusually realistic provision was made for the reculturing of the teachers who would ultimately be expected to implement new teaching approaches in their classroom, no provision at all was made for those they had left behind, leading to the problems outlined in 6.3.1.2 above when they returned to their home environments.

This is a reminder that successful implementation of any such change depends fundamentally not only on how *teachers* think and behave, but also on the thinking and behaviour of a range of other people within and outside the education system. The more complex the change is, the more essential it is that national and local change leaders spend time at the implementation-planning stage considering who will be affected and how they can be helped to understand the main features of the change, why it is desirable and the part they can play in supporting it.

### 6.4.2 The components that affect the teaching of any subject are interconnected

This case also re-emphasizes the need for national policy makers to remember and take account of the interconnectedness of the various components that influence the teaching of any subject. Planning how to train teachers in the 'what', 'why' and 'how' of whatever change it is hoped to implement, is clearly one very important aspect of any change process. However, again, teachers are not the only influence on what happens in classrooms. As the returning teachers discovered, exams (and also materials) can be just as influential, and lack of harmony between teacher training, teaching approach, materials and exams will make change-implementation more difficult.

There seem often to be political, practical and/or economic reasons that make it difficult for all components to be made simultaneously consistent with the proposed change. If that is so, as in the current case, any teacher training needs to explicitly recognize this, since it has implications for the content of the training. For example, in the above case, textbooks and exams were not changed to 'fit' the new teaching approaches. It would have been helpful, therefore, for teacher trainers to have spent time with trainees developing strategies for using the textbooks they were already familiar with in different ways, to try to enable them to give their learners at least some of the learning experiences appropriate for a more communicative approach.

### 6.4.3 Legislating for change does not mean it happens

The mistaken notion that plans for change officially announced on paper inevitably translate to their implementation in classrooms is again suggested here. Even though detailed planning for dissemination was non-existent, there still seemed to be an assumption that trainees would return to their working environments and have an effect (a positive effect in the sense of the contributing to the desired outcome of a new teaching approach) on colleagues in the local area.

### 6.4.4 The more deeply entrenched an educational culture is, the longer any significant reculturing process will take

The complexity of an educational change depends partly on the degree of personal and/or professional adjustment that those involved need to make in order to move from existing behaviours and understandings to those needed to begin implementation. A further factor that will affect the rate and route of change within an educational setting is the depth and strength of the existing educational culture. In this case, some aspects of the educational culture (particularly the expected roles of teachers and learners in classrooms) were very longstanding, and were therefore deeply etched into people's 'key meanings' (see chapter 1.3) In such circumstances an educational change that demands a degree of reculturing is likely to take even longer to reach the continuation stage where the 'change' becomes a new cultural norm. In addition, where such a deeply seated existing culture exists, it becomes particularly important for national and local policy makers to plan for implementation in a manner that tries to provide a degree of 'cultural continuity' (Holliday op cit). This may mean planning for implementation in stages that allow 'bridges' to be built between the status quo and the proposed educational change. In this context, an example of such a bridge might have been to plan first to introduce new techniques and types of activity related to the teaching of reading, since dealing with text was already something that all teachers and learners were familiar with.

Chapter 7

# Introducing a new subject in primary school

## 7.1 The background to the change

This case is a further example of educational change that was introduced to meet a perceived need for the outcomes of the national education system to better meet the demands of a rapidly changing wider world. Over the past two decades national policy makers in many countries have considered an adequate level of proficiency in English to be an increasingly important educational outcome for learners in their state systems. In many countries on all continents dissatisfaction with the existing outcomes of English teaching have led policy makers to decide that the learning of English should begin earlier. This case is an example of one such decision to move to introduce English, previously taught only in secondary schools, at primary level.

Again, the education system involved was highly centralized, top down and hierarchical. The change was introduced without wide national consultation, with local-educational planners/administrators instructed by the centre to ensure that English began to be taught in the third year of all the primary schools for which they were responsible by a set date. A very general outline curriculum was provided for each of the two 'levels' at primary school, and it was officially stated that English should not be formally assessed. The case reported on here discusses the first stages of one region's attempt to try to prepare to implement this national policy. The case reports on a two-year period covering the planning for, and very early implementation of, the national change in one region of the country. The actual implementation process continues to the present day.

## 7.2 The initiation/planning stage

### 7.2.1 Leadership timing and funding

The timescale that national policy makers gave for the introduction of English at primary level was about two years. This may seem quite a long time. However, the majority of primary schools had never offered English (although some in big cities already did), and there were therefore few primary English teacher trainers, few primary English teachers and few primary English materials. There was also little understanding of the rationale for the change or its implications for teaching approaches among most of those leading, working in, or attending primary schools or among parents in the wider society. There was therefore a lot to do in the time available

Policy makers in the case study region recognized the need to plan for implementation in this context. Given the magnitude of the task, they decided to begin by trying to deal with one of the most fundamental of the above shortages.

---

QUESTION TO CONSIDER

If you were responsible for beginning preparations to implement this change, where would you start?

---

Regional policy makers chose to begin by developing a group of primary English trainer-trainers, who would understand the main differences between Teaching English to Young Learners (TEYL) and teaching teenagers or adults, understand what classroom conditions were needed to support TEYL and be familiar with some key techniques for enabling such learning to take place. Members of this group would then, it was originally planned, be available to provide both further trainer- training and teacher training and so enable the region to rapidly expand the number of primary English teachers. It was decided that the initial training of the core trainer-trainer groups would last three months and would take place at a British university with recognized expertise in TEYL.

The case-study region was relatively prosperous. Policy makers recognized that the trainer-training programme would require both on-going funding and their continuing involvement in the planning of the trainer-training project, its implementation and in how trainers would be used thereafter. You will probably have noticed that in this case the commitment to ongoing leadership involvement at both planning and implementation stages represents a contrast to the two previous studies.

### 7.2.2 Understanding the national and local change context

The region involved in this case had very uneven social and economic development. Parts of the region were well developed and economically affluent, and in some schools in some urban areas primary English teaching had already been provided for several years. Other parts of the region, the majority, were more representative of the picture outlined at 7.2.1 above. It was recognized by regional planners that if the UK trainer-training programme was to be of value, it was important for the UK side to have some sense of context, and so a one-week, baseline study visit was made by a member of staff from the project university.

Such baseline studies, in which information can be gathered about existing realities in the proposed change context to inform planning, do, as I have previously mentioned, have great potential value, even if they are only short and relatively superficial. The visit in this case enabled factual information about the proposed implementation to be gathered, for example what number of primary teachers will need training, how many hours of English teaching per week there will be, and whether and how it will be assessed. It was also an opportunity to obtain examples of primary textbooks that were already being used, and the outline primary curriculum and other relevant documents. However, the value of such studies can be greatly diminished if, as often happens for understandable but unhelpful reasons when outsiders are involved, the contexts that the baseline study uses as its baseline are examples of existing 'best practice' rather than examples of conditions in more typical baseline institutions. This was the case here.

---

QUESTIONS TO CONSIDER

What relevant contextual information was such a baseline-study visit likely to miss?

What effects might the lack of accurate contextual information have on the design and/or content of proposed trainer-training programme and/or the wider implementation process?

---

Some of the contextual information that was missed was a sense of the:

- class sizes that most teachers would be working with
- conditions in most classrooms in terms of space and flexibility of seating
- resources that would be available to support teaching in most schools
- extent to which there was awareness of the change among school leaders and parents and/or whether it would be welcomed when it was implemented
- pressure that there would be to formally assess English learning
- extent to which generally accepted TEYL activities and techniques would conflict with the existing primary-school educational culture

Lack of such information might result in the proposed trainer-training programme, for example:

- spending time introducing, discussing and practising TEYL teaching approaches techniques and activities that would not, for practical or cultural reasons, be feasible in normal classroom conditions, instead of working with trainers to think about how the most important ideas could be adapted to become possible to implement in a range of likely classroom realities
- spending too little time developing simple explanations of the rationale for TEYL and its main classroom principles, and developing/practising ways of

presenting them to teachers, local-level administrators, school leaders and/or parents

For reasons of partial ignorance on the part of the UK training providers, and perhaps reluctance to highlight the scale and complexity of what region-wide implementation implied on the part of the regional policy makers, important aspects of the context were not sufficiently considered at the planning stage. This affected the design of the trainer-training programme, which then in turn affected the extent to which the teacher training that was provided by trainers on their return could actually be implemented (see 7.3.1.2 below).

## 7.2.3 Clarity of expectations

The concrete expectation of the national change was that by a given date all primary schools would be offering at least some English teaching to all learners. What this concrete expectation would in fact mean in classroom practice was of course far less clear, given the very sketchy curriculum guidelines provided by national policy makers and the variations in existing primary-school English-teaching practice and understanding between and within the different regions. As in previous cases, national policy makers seemed content to introduce the official change and then 'require' lower levels of the organizational/administrative hierarchy to develop concrete plans for implementation.

At the regional level the expectations expressed by the leadership were that the trainers who went to the UK should study for a formal accredited university qualification and should be able to train others in TEYL when they returned.

---

QUESTION TO CONSIDER
What advantages and disadvantages might there be to linking a context-specific training course to an existing formal academic qualification?

---

- A perceived advantage, which strongly influenced the regional planners, was a sense that the qualification would increase the value they were obtaining for their substantial financial investment. First, linking the training to a qualification would motivate participants to take the training seriously, since failure to achieve the qualification would be clearly visible, and so embarrassing. Second, having a formal qualification would add to the trainers' credibility on their return, and so help make it more likely that they would be taken seriously when providing training to others.
- A disadvantage, which became clear during the actual provision of the training, was that the need to teach towards a qualification constrained what was and was not possible during the training. Significant time had to be spent on developing the academic skills needed to complete the written assignments against which successful achievement of the qualification would be judged. Such time might have been better used developing more practical professional training skills.

Apart from the desire that trainers should obtain a recognized qualification, there was no clarity at the initial planning stage about exactly how the trainers would be used when they returned. There was an assumption that they would train others in the principles of TEYL, but who would be trained, when and where they would be trained, how long the training would be and how it would be structured were not clear. More definite decisions regarding trainers' post-return roles were made once the first (of four) groups were actually in the UK. These decisions remained unchanged for the later groups, and so could be taken account of by the training institution when working with later groups.

The UK training institution had considerable experience of working with international colleagues, and the content of the Certificate programme that the trainers were to follow was more or less defined. It was planned that study for the Certificate would run over two of the three months, with the final month being spent on the development of TEYL training materials and on trainer-training. There was, however, concern on the part of both the regional leaders and the UK institution about ensuring that most participants would be people whose existing roles had some sort of a training remit within the existing regional or local structure and would therefore be appropriately situated to 'train' on their return. In addition, since they would be studying for an accredited and assessed qualification, it was necessary that their English language should be at a level that would allow them to do so.

In order to be able to select appropriate participants, it was therefore agreed that the UK institution would provide two two-week introductory courses in the change environment. Over 100 possible participants would attend each. Face-to-face interaction with, and observation of, participants, together with information on the above two criteria, provided an approximate sense of who seemed to be suited for the longer training programme. Most eventual participants were therefore either existing local-level teacher trainers, trainers from colleges specializing in the training of primary teachers or primary teachers considered to have trainer potential. Although there were representatives from all parts of the region, the majority came from the more-developed areas and had some prior TEYL experience.

### 7.2.4 Conclusion

Compared to the two previous cases, the regional leadership in this case did take an active interest in the planning of the trainer-training initiative that they hoped would provide significant support for the implementation of national policy.

However, in two main areas here too the planning process had important gaps. First, although the partial baseline study that was carried out was worth doing, the fact that it did not really investigate the full 'baseline' meant that it failed to register a number of important contextual issues that would later negatively affect the implementation process. Second, although it did quite soon become clear how the trainers would be used immediately after their return home, there was no real planning of how they might be used over time to support the on-going implementation process region-wide. This, as will be seen below, resulted in the under-utilization of a potentially significant resource.

## 7.3 The implementation of the change

### 7.3.1 Matching change to local realities

I discuss this aspect of the change-implementation process from two points of view. The first relates to the trainer-training aspect of the case study. The second considers the extent to which the training offered by trainers on their return was appropriate to the local realities of the primary teachers being trained.

### 7.3.1.1 The trainer training

As discussed above, the insistence that the training should be linked to a formal qualification meant that more time needed to be spent on issues relating to the academic aspects than would otherwise have been necessary. Nonetheless, this was an essentially practical qualification, which over the first two months discussed the main principles underlying the teaching of languages to young learners, the rationale for these and demonstrated and practised some of the most widely used classroom techniques and activities for operationalizing such principles. The course of study tried to make connections to local realities as far as it was able, for example through reference to participants' prior experiences of their context and the use of local textbooks. However, due both to lack of time and lack of baseline information, this part of the programme was not able to spend sufficient time on considering the implications of contextual realities on what was being learned in any detail.

The final month of the programme had two main foci. By the time the first group had reached this point, the regional planners had decided that each returning group would be responsible for running a three-week training pro-gramme for up to 800 existing and potential primary-school English teachers in whatever holiday period followed their return. The first focus was therefore to develop a set of training materials that they could use on such programmes. The second was to help them develop training skills that would enable them to use the training materials as effectively as possible. This dual focus represented an enor-mous demand, especially for the first group of trainers who had to design the training materials from scratch.

> QUESTION TO CONSIDER
> If you had been a member of this first group of trainers, on what would you have based the design of such materials?

Unsurprisingly the first group of trainers returned first to the notes, handouts, readings and examples of materials and activities that they had gathered during the previous two months, to serve as a basis for their training materials. These had been designed for the purpose of helping trainers understand the theory and practice of TEYL. They were not, especially in an undigested and unadapted form, necessarily appropriate for the three-week training course that the trainers would be expected to provide for teachers from all over the region on their return. However, given the time constraints on the first group, and their need to produce training materials together with necessary handouts, textbook examples and visuals for use with teachers very shortly after they returned, they naturally used the resources that were most immediately available. For the first group, most of the time during the last month had to be spent preparing materials to a very tight deadline. Too little time was available for discussing and practising how, as trainers, they might best organize and manage the presentation of ideas, the opportunities for discussion, the personal modelling and the teacher practice of TEYL activities that the materials offered. The three groups that followed were more fortunate in two ways. First, they were able to use this first draft set of training materials as a starting point for adaptation. Second, by the time they came to the UK, almost all of them had already had experience of using the materials/ seeing the materials in use on real training programmes (see 7.3.2.2). Consequently they were also able to spend more time developing and practising trainer skills.

Over time the staff working on the UK training course also became aware of more aspects of the trainers' realities. Through participation in the teacher-training programmes (see below) staff had greater exposure to what the trainers were being expected to do on their return (the training context in terms of numbers, facilities, intensity, prior knowledge of participants), the aspects of training that they found most difficult, and the classroom reality of the teachers whom they were training. Given the constraints outlined above, such under-standings affected both the 'what' and the 'how' of subsequent cycles of the UK-based training.

### 7.3.1.2 The TEYL teacher training

The whole purpose of the trainer-training was of course to enable the provision of the TEYL teacher training that would in turn enable the regional planners to meet the demands of national educational policy. The form that this teacher training took was a series of teacher-training programmes arranged for the summer and winter holidays immediately following the return home of each group of trainers. Each programme was residential over three weeks, with 12 working days spent on the formal training. Each programme had approximately 800 teachers divided into 20–25 classes of 30–40 teachers. Each trainer was responsible for one class. In order to lessen the burden, and more importantly to provide future trainers with exposure to the training process, trainers from subsequent groups were expected to attend the programme immediately prior to their departure for the UK, to work as an assistant to one of the newly returned trainers. In addition, to provide further support to the trainers and to gain first-hand experience of the teacher-training context, two staff members from the UK training programme also participated in each training programme.

The programme content was based on the materials developed by the trainers during their time in the UK. These materials were in turn based on the content of the UK programme, albeit increasingly adjusted over time in terms of weighting, examples and materials in the light of experience. TEYL theory is based on ideas about how children learn, how they learn language and what characteristics common to children everywhere imply for the sorts of activities that help them learn. Some of the principles introduced in the teacher-training programme were therefore likely to be broadly familiar to any participant who had been trained in the teaching of, or had experience of working with, young children. The outline national curriculum also supported many of the principles of TEYL by emphasizing the need for English learning in primary school to focus on activities that, for example, asked children to use English to play games, listen to stories, sing songs, or watch cartoons without the stress of being subjected to formal assessment.

However, the educational culture of which teachers attending the programme were part (together with their school leaders, their colleagues, their learners and their learners' parents) remained towards the transmission end of the continuum proposed in Figure 3.1 (see page 33). This meant that language learning at all levels was viewed as a process that must involve learning tangible knowledge and being assessed on the this learning, which in the case of language meant grammar and vocabulary. A three-week training programme could not alone hope to completely change such beliefs and their associated teaching behaviours.

In 7.2.2 above I mentioned some of the features of the primary-teaching contest that the baseline study had failed to identify. A short survey (Wedell 2005) responded to by 511 of the teachers attending the third teacher-training programme, showed that these features did for many teachers represent barriers to the local implementation of the less formal, meaning-focused and activity-centred teaching approach that was introduced in the training programme. The teachers were first asked whether they thought that the techniques/activities for developing young learners' language skills that had been introduced during the training could be used in their primary English classrooms – 98.2 per cent of them said yes. They were then asked whether there were any factors (apart from their own lack of experience or lack of confidence) that might make it difficult to use these techniques/activities in their classroom, and 85 per cent said yes. Those answering yes were requested to list up to three of the most important factors. The reasons given by more than 10 per cent of teachers are summarized in Table 7.1.

The table shows the answers to some questions about local contexts that the baseline study failed to ask, and which it would have been useful for those offering the UK training to know. If this information had been available it might have been possible to make a stronger case for not linking the training to an accredited qualification, instead using more of the available time to discuss and practise ways of implementing important TEYL principles in typical classroom contexts. Such a focus would in turn have been reflected in the structure and content of the teacher

**Table 7.1**   Teachers' perceptions of factors making it difficult to use techniques/ activities introduced during training in primary classrooms.

| Factors making it difficult to implement training techniques/activities | Number/percentage of respondents (100% = 511) |
|---|---|
| 1. Class size; large numbers, the difficulty of managing large numbers, physical space. | 245 47.9% |
| 2. The small number of lessons per week and the pressure to 'finish the book' to meet the demands of the test, both making it difficult to find the time needed to use suggested techniques/activities. | 181 35.4% |
| 3. Incompatibility of testing content/format with the use of techniques/activities and the critical role of test results in leaders' judgements of students' and teachers' performance. | 92 18% |
| 4. Learners' language level and inability to understand meanings and instructions, and their cultural reluctance to participate. | 84 16.4% |
| 5. Inappropriacy of textbooks, and so shortage of materials to support the use of suggested activities. | 77 15.1% |
| 6. Teachers' excessive workloads, and so their lack of time to plan classes and materials that incorporate these techniques/activities. | 74 14.5% |
| 7. A general lack of understanding of/interest in the purpose or process of language learning in the school and immediate outside environment. | 58 11.3% |

Source: Adapted from Wedell 2005: 641.

training materials, and would probably also have influenced what aspects of trainer development were emphasized. Instead the teacher training programmes, while introducing teachers to a range of primary language teaching activities that most of them found relevant, did not sufficiently acknowledge or take account of aspects of the local context that might make them difficult for many teachers to use.

## 7.3.2 Support for learning the 'what' and 'how' of change

At first glance the trainer-training programme and the teacher-training programmes that followed did provide support for trainers and teachers to be introduced to some of the 'whats' and 'hows' of the national change that they would be expected to implement. However, considered more carefully, both sets of training provided just an initial introduction to the new understandings and skills that would be needed. Such an introduction alone was not sufficient to enable widespread confident or competent implementation.

The only explicit expectation of the trainers was that they should work on one teacher-training programme after their return. While a minority did work on more than one programme, and many of them had explicit training roles in their existing jobs, there was no structure to provide support for them to develop their training skills further once the teacher-training programmes ended. The trainer training they had received emphasized the need for trainers, for example, to:

- begin by finding out about teachers' previous experiences, and their existing beliefs and behaviours, in order, wherever possible, to make links between these and whatever new ideas/practices were to be implemented
- help teachers understand new practices and be able to explain their value to others
- provide opportunities for teachers to experience and think about new ideas and activities themselves, through trainer demonstrations, before expecting them to apply them
- provide teachers with opportunities to practise planning and managing new techniques and activities, and chances to think about and obtain reactions to such practise from peers and trainers (adapted from Hayes 2000)

The trainer training aimed to develop a responsive and flexible mode of training. This was very different from the tightly structured, lecture-based training approach most commonly used in the context. Developing competence at, and confidence in, approaching the training process in such a flexible and responsive manner takes time and plenty of practice. Many trainers found their one experience of being expected to train in such a different manner extremely difficult and were probably pleased not to have to repeat it! A significant minority, however, found it exciting. For those trainers who wished to develop further, the lack of explicit further opportunities to train and/or support teachers after their return (see below), represented an under-utilization of the investment that regional planners had made in their training.

Similarly, turning to the teachers, once again support for their further development was lacking. A single teacher-training programme carried out away from participants' teaching context does not result in teachers who are immediately able to implement the content of the training in their own classrooms. Research into teacher learning and teacher change from around the world (Dalin 1994; Fullan 2000; Harvey 1996, 1999; Lamb 1995; Leithwood et al. 2002; Li 1998; Showers and Joyce 1996) testifies to the need for continuing support for teachers over time, especially where, as is often the case, and was true here, the initial training does not fully acknowledge important aspects of the classroom realities in which most teachers work.

If regional policy makers had been willing to carry out a more truly representative baseline study, it would have demonstrated some of the obvious difficulties that class size, limited time and lack of appropriate materials would represent for the implementation of TEYL in many classrooms. This information would, as said previously, have been useful for those providing trainer training and designing teacher-training materials. It might also have reminded planners of the need to plan for and fund mechanisms to help teachers returning from training programmes, and their larger number of untrained colleagues, to collaborate and support each other during the early years of introducing English into primary classrooms.

The first case (chapter 5) showed how positively implementers in different institutions viewed the opportunities that were provided for them to meet each other and share problems and solutions. One way of meeting the above need might therefore have been to plan for the establishment of some form of primary English teachers' group in each district, town or county represented on the teacher-training programmes. To provide a nucleus for the formation of such groups, regional planners could have arranged for each administrative area to send a minimum of two or three of their teachers to one of the training courses. The two years during which the trainer and teacher training took place could have been used to publicize and promote the formation of such groups as teachers returned from the three-week courses to their areas. Since funding would be necessary to set up, facilitate and maintain such groups, policy makers could have agreed to offer like-for-like funding to any local-level educational administrators willing to provide matching funding, a space for meetings and time for regular meetings within school hours.

Such planning would potentially also have enabled the greater utilization of the minority of trainers who were keen to develop their training skills. Those who wished to might for example have been seconded for a period of time (taking account of their personal circumstances) to act as expert 'coaches' (Joyce and Showers 1988; Showers and Joyce 1996) or trainers of coaches for the local-level teachers' groups suggested above, as well as perhaps disseminating teacher training more widely through further, smaller-scale, local teacher-training programmes.

### 7.3.3 Leadership of the change-implementation process

The previous section may suggest that there was a lack of leadership during the planning and early years of the TEYL implementation process covered by this case study. This would however only be partly true. While policy makers failed to consider some aspects of the reality of the overall implementation context, within the limited boundaries of the case, whose focus was on enabling some sort of implementation to begin with teachers who were at least partly prepared, they were actively involved. They managed the logistics and funding of the teacher-training programmes, they ensured that returning trainers attended these and enabled subsequent trainers to attend as assistants. They kept closely in touch with the UK training institution and monitored the performance of trainers in the UK. Finally they strongly encouraged representatives of all four groups to collaborate on turning the training materials that they had developed into a TEYL handbook for the region. This was duly published. Overall, therefore, compared with the national-change leaders in both other cases discussed, the regional leadership in this case were highly participative and involved.

## 7.4 What does this case tell us about the educational-change process?

### 7.4.1 It may be wise for national educational changes to be introduced in only very general terms

National policy makers' decision to introduce English at primary level was not accompanied by much detailed guidance as to the content or process of such new learning. I do not know the reasons for this but it seems a wise decision. Given the very great contextual differences across the country in terms of socio-economic level and prior experience of the change, it would have been impossible to provide detailed universal guidance for the stages of implementation and therefore a general directive to start the process was probably all that could realistically be provided. This represents a positive example of pragmatic willingness to allow local leaders to plan implementation in a manner that is appropriate for them.

However, for such a devolved model of implementation to lead to positive outcomes across a country, it is necessary for local leaders to be helped to thoroughly understand what is being asked of them and to be fairly funded. In the case-study setting, the local leaders in a rapidly modernizing, well-developed region were able to take appropriate initiatives without detailed guidance from above. The region was also sufficiently economically developed to be able to fund the trainer-training and teacher-training programmes. The situation in other parts of the country was less favourable.

### 7.4.2 Change policy that ignores powerful cultural, social or material realities will not achieve its hoped-for outcomes

The national policy documents relating to the teaching of English at primary level explicitly stated that there should not be formal assessment of learners. It became clear during the baseline study that this was ignored in schools that had already begun primary English. Assessment might remain informal for the very early primary years, but since for most ambitious parents, especially in urban areas, primary schools were merely the stepping-stone to their child's entry to a 'good' secondary school, and since such secondary schools had traditional form-focused English entrance exams, formal assessment of a very traditional kind was common in the last few years of primary school. The inevitable effect in many cases was to orient English teaching during these years firmly towards the formal study of language. This diminished the chance of achieving one of the hoped-for outcomes of a longer period of language study, the development of a positive attitude to, and enjoyment of, using English among learners. Policy makers cannot have been unaware that this would be so.

Similarly, regional policy makers in the case-study setting cannot have been unaware of the material and cultural reality that would influence what teachers perceive as possible in the classroom. As shown above, ignoring these influenced the impact of both the trainer-training and the teacher-training provision.

This suggests that policy makers, when planning for implementation:

- will almost certainly fail to obtain the most effective return on their investment of time and resources if their plans do not consider at least the most typically occurring contextual factors that may influence the success of what it is hoped to achieve
- are likely to lessen the chance of implementers viewing the proposed change positively if it becomes evident that their plans for supporting the implementation process do not in fact take such day to day contextual factors into account
- should be frank with whomever they delegate the provision of support programmes to, so that they are aware of all important contextual factors and can design and teach such programmes bearing these in mind

### 7.4.3 A single 'change' training course, away from the working context, is almost certainly insufficient to enable a complex change to be implemented as hoped

As repeatedly mentioned, and as I hope the previous case illustrated, complex change is just that. For individuals (teachers, trainers or administrators) to become able to develop understanding of, and confidence in, their ability to practise what it actually entails in their own classrooms or offices, a long time is required (remember that the teachers in chapter 6 had two years of full-time training!).

Policy makers at all levels therefore need to:

- consider whether large-scale training away from the classroom in which the training will be implemented is the most useful way of supporting implementation
- recognize that if they choose this means of introducing the change to teachers, they will need to develop systems to provide ongoing support for teachers working in their own classrooms after the initial training course is over

### 7.4.4 Trained teachers are only *part* of any successful educational change process

As in the previous cases, it is clear here that while choosing to *start* a change planning process by trying to ensure that most teachers have at least an outline understanding of what is expected of them may make sense, this is just one aspect of the whole change context. Other aspects cannot be ignored.

# Conclusion to section 2

The three case studies that I have reported here all represent elements of larger educational-change processes that have not yet been fully completed. They span twenty years. The first trainees were recruited to case-two training in the late 1980s and the last in the late 1990s. Case one ran throughout most of the 1990s and case three began in the early noughties and continues to the present. In this final part of the chapter, I briefly summarize some of the themes that I feel all cases share.

## 1 The approach to the planning of change

In all the cases, the change planning is undeniably top down and implicitly, at least, power coercive in Chin and Benne's terms. National-level policy makers reach their decisions without wide consultation, especially with those who will be expected to carry out the actual implementation. They make little effort to communicate the rationale for change and the main benefits that it is expected to bring about and provide only very sketchy guidance as to what the change outcomes ought to look like, or how those to whom they have delegated responsibility for implementation should begin to think about the process. There seems to be an assumption that the top needs only to 'require' that regional, local or institutional leaders act, and they will know what to do. As is hopefully clear, they often do not know. Such an approach does not lead to success.

## 2 Policy makers' unawareness of context

Perhaps because of their top-down organizational culture, policy makers at all levels in all the above cases seemed to underestimate the criticality of at least considering contextual reality in their planning. Relevant aspects of such reality include:

- the material context of their existing education systems, for example the class sizes or the facilities available
- the socio-economic context, for example teachers' salaries and status within society
- the geographical context, for example the economic and social disparities that exist between different parts of the country
- the human context, for example the assumptions prevailing among educators, administrators, learners and parents in the existing educational and organizational cultures

## 3 Educational change as complex change involving a degree of 'reculturing'

Education systems all around the world are deeply traditional and many seem only now to be beginning to seriously contemplate the content and process of education as involving more than the transmission of a body of mostly fact-based knowledge from one generation to the next. There is of course a growing body of educational rhetoric visible in policy documents worldwide that use terms like *learner-centred classrooms*, *learner autonomy*, *interaction*, *enquiry-based learning* or *developing learners' problem-solving skills*. However, assumptions about appropriate teaching roles and behaviours visible among participants at all levels in the cases suggest that a basically transmission-based view of education remains very influential.

If this is so then any educational change that hopes to lead to genuinely different learner outcomes is likely to involve complex changes to existing educational and organizational cultures. Achieving successful implementation will require many people's commitment over time. Sustained commitment requires appropriate support. Top-down, power-coercive approaches are unlikely to be able to provide such support. If there is ever to be widespread successful implementation of complex educational change, policy makers need to reassess the manner in which they approach the planning and managing of such change.

## 4 Policy makers are inconsistent

In each of the cases there was evidence of inconsistency between what changed and what did not. For example, while curricula or teaching approach officially changed, approaches to teacher education, the content of teaching materials and, most influentially, the content and format of high-stakes tests did not. Again there may be a number for reasons for this, from lack of awareness of the mutual manner in which different aspects of any subject area influence each other, to lack of funding to renew the textbooks, to the political difficulties that are inherent in changing something as sensitive as a university entrance exam. Nonetheless, such inconsistency makes change implementation difficult, if not impossible, in the short term.

## 5 Educational change is often a response to other changes in the national or international environment

The cases all show evidence of educational change policy being affected by actual or perceived changes in either the national or international environments. In an increasingly interdependent world, in which countries compete for shares of an ever more global market, and so become increasingly aware of the need to have a skilled work force, such trends are likely to continue.

## 6 Educational changes focus almost exclusively on the teacher

It is not surprising that teachers are seen to be central to the implementation of any educational change. They are. However, as all the cases showed, in order for teachers to feel that the implementation efforts they are asked to make are worthwhile over the years that developing new mastery can take, they need to feel that the wider educational environment, and those outside whom it influences, are all broadly supportive of the change and understand what the teachers are trying to do. For this to be so, educational-change planners need to become far more aware of all the others who require 'change education'; not only teachers, but also those who affect their view of themselves and of the work they do.

The importance of some sort of 'baseline study' to provide a real sense of the context into which the change is to be introduced, prior to beginning detailed planning of change implementation in a local area, has been referred to in this chapter. The lack of such information also contributed to the problems that were encountered in the other cases discussed. Carrying out a formal, systematic, study nationwide is a complex, time-consuming, and so expensive, business. Hence it rarely happens. However at local level I believe strongly that even if carried out only quickly and cheaply such studies can provide information that can positively inform the implementation planning process. The final section of the book therefore proposes a small number of key questions that might guide such studies. I then ask and answer these questions in three different educational-change scenarios to demonstrate what the information that the answers provide implies for the sequence and timing of the change-planning and change-implementation processes.

## References

### Works cited

Carey, T. and Dabor, M. (1995), 'Management Education: An approach to improved language teaching', *English Language Teaching Journal*, 49/1, 37–43.

Dalin, P. (1994), *How Schools Improve*. London: IMTEC.

Fullan, M.G. (1991), 'Planning, doing and coping with change' in A. Harris, N. Bennett and M. Preedy (eds), *Organisational Effectiveness and Improvement in Education*, 205-218. Buckingham: Open University Press.

Fullan, M.G. (2000), 'The return of large-scale reform', *Journal of Educational Change*, 1, 5–28.

Harvey, S.P. (1996), 'Primary science', inset in 'South Africa: an evaluation of classroom support', unpublished PhD thesis. University of Exeter.

Harvey, S.P. (1999), 'The impact of coaching in South African primary science', inset in *International Journal of Educational Development*, 19/3, 191-205.

Hayes, D. (2000), 'Cascade training and teachers' professional development', *English Language Teaching Journal*, 54/2, 135–45.

Horvath, A. (1990), 'Tradition and modernism: Educational consequences of changes in Hungarian society', *International Review of Education*, 36/2, 207–17.

Lamb, M.V. (1995), 'The consequences of', inset in *English Language Teaching Journal*, 49/1, 72–79.

Leithwood, K., Jantzi, D. and Mascall, B. (2002), 'A framework for research on large-scale reform', *Journal of Educational Change*, 3, 7–33.

Li, Defeng (1998), 'It's always more difficult than you plan and imagine: teachers' perceived difficulties in introducing the communicative approach in South Korea', in D.R. Hall and A. Hewings (eds), *Innovation in English Language Teaching*, 149–66. London: Routledge.

Malderez, A. and Wedell, M. (2007), *Teaching Teachers: Processes and Practices*. London: Continuum.

Medgyes, P. and Malderez, A. (eds) (1996), *Changing Pespectives in Teacher Education*. Oxford: Heinemann.

Ouyang, H.H. (2000), 'One way ticket: a story of an innovative teacher in mainland China', *Anthropology & Education Quarterly*, 31/4, 397–425.

Showers, B. and Joyce, B. (1996), 'The evolution of peer coaching', *Educational Leadership*, 53, 12–16.

Wedell, M. (2000), 'Managing educational change in a turbulent environment: the ELTSUP project in Hungary 1991-1998', unpublished PhD thesis. University of Glamorgan.

Wedell, M. (2005), 'Cascading training down into the classroom: The need for parallel planning', *International Journal of Educational Development*, 25/6, 637–651.

## Further Reading

There are a large number of books and articles dealing with the experiences of those involved in educational-change initiatives relating to the teaching of English in different countries. Most such initiatives have been related to curriculum change, and the move from a broadly transmission-based approach to the teaching of language to a more 'communicative' approach, such as the one referred to in chapters 5 and 6 in this section. These change initiatives have therefore been complex, since they have involved a considerable degree of reculturing. Few, if any, have been unambiguously successful, for reasons similar to those discussed in the case studies.

### Books

Holliday, A. (1994), *Appropriate Methodology and Social Context*. Cambridge: Cambridge University Press.

This was one of the first books to explicitly recognize the need to consider cultural contexts when introducing educational change. Its focus is on an educational-change programme in Egypt.

Coleman, H. (ed.) (1996), *Society and the Language Classroom*. Cambridge: Cambridge University Press.

This edited edition contains examples of responses to culturally different teaching approaches from China, Japan, Pakistan and Indonesia, together with a very clear table demonstrating how different views of education impact on expected teacher and learner roles and on what happens in classrooms.

Kennedy, C., Doyle, P. and Goh, C. (eds) (1999), *Exploring Change in English Language Teaching*. Oxford: Macmillan/Heinemann.

This discusses attempts to implement national-change initiatives in Malaysia and Hong Kong.

Hall, D.R. and Hewings, A. (eds) (2001), *Innovation in English Language Teaching*. London: Routledge.

This introduces the idea of the need for cultural continuity in any educational-change initiative and also examples of change initiatives from South Korea and Pakistan.

*Articles*

The first group of articles discuss approaches to, or frameworks for, the leadership/management of educational change, and/or discuss factors in the wider context, which may influence the route or rate of educational change implementation.

Dushku, S. (1998), 'ELT in Albania: project evaluation and change', *System*, 26/3, 369–88.
Huh, K.C. (2001), 'Is finding the right balance with regard to change possible, given the tensions that occur between global influences and local traditions in countries in Asia-Pacific?', *Journal of Educational Change*, 2, 257–60.
Kennedy, C. (1988), 'Evaluating the management of change', *Applied Linguistics*, 9/4, 329–42.
Luxon, T. (1994), 'The psychological risk for teachers at a time of methodological change', *Teacher Trainer*, 8/1, 6–9.
Nunan, D. (2003), 'The impact of English as a global language on educational policies and practices in the Asia-Pacific region', *TESOL Quarterly*, 37/4, 589–613.
Tudor, I. (2003), 'Learning to live with complexity: towards an ecological perspective on language teaching', *System*, 31/1, 1–12.
Waters, A. and Vilches, M. (2001), 'Implementing ELT innovations: a needs analysis framework', *English Language Teaching Journal*, 55/2, 133–141.
Wedell, M. (2003), 'Giving TESOL change a chance: supporting key players in the curriculum change process', *System*, 31/4, 439–56.

The second group are more like case studies and report on aspects of (usually) teachers' experience of participating in English-language-teaching-related change initiatives around the world.

Al Hamzi, S. (2003), 'EFL teacher preparation programmes in Saudi Arabia: trends and challenges', *TESOL Quarterly*, 37/2, 341–45.
Berry, R.S.Y. (2003), 'English language teaching and learning in mainland China: a comparison of the intentions of the English language curriculum reform and the

real life teaching and learning situation in the English classroom', *Hong Kong Institute of Education NAS Newsletter*, 4, 3–6.

Butler, Y.G. (2004), 'What level of English proficiency do elementary school teachers need to attain to teach EFL? Case studies from Korea, Taiwan and Japan', *TESOL Quarterly*, 38/2, 245–78.

Chacon, C.T. (2005), 'Teachers perceived efficacy among English as a foreign language teachers in middle schools in Venezuela', *Teaching and Teacher Education*, 21, 257–72.

Hyde, B. (1994), 'Albanian babies and bathwater', *Teacher Trainer*, 8/1, 10–13.

Hu, G.W. (2002), 'Recent important developments in secondary English language teaching in the P.R. China', *Language Culture and Curriculum*, 15/1, 30–49.

Orafi, S. (2008), 'Investigating teachers' practices and beliefs in relation to curriculum innovation in ELT in Libya', unpublished PhD thesis. University of Leeds.

Prophet, R. (1995), 'View from the Botswana Junior Secondary classroom: case study of a curriculum intervention', *International Journal of Educational Development*, 15/2, 127–40.

Waters, A. (with Ma. Luz C. Vilches) (2008), 'Factors affecting ELT reforms: the case of the Philippines basic education curriculum', *RELC Journal*, 39/1, 5–24.

Wu, X.D. and Fang, L. (2002), 'Teaching communicative English in China: a case study of the gap between teachers' views and practice', *Asian Journal of ELT*, 12, 143–162.

# Planning to Implement Educational Change: Beginning at the beginning

# Introduction

I imagine that by now you will not need convincing about how complicated the process of planning to implement almost any educational change is likely to be. You will also, I hope, recognize that even when apparently implemented successfully, a change can take many years to reach a point where it becomes just another part of normal classroom life. For example, one complex change in education systems worldwide during the last 10–15 years that most of you will have encountered in some form is the introduction of information and communications technology (ICT) into education systems worldwide at all levels. The rationale for the massive financial investment that this represents has been the assumption that the use of technology will enable changes to teaching and learning practices in school classrooms, which will in turn enable learners to benefit from a far more flexible, interactive, challenging and personalized learning experience. Such hoped-for changes in teaching and learning behaviour of course presuppose a greater or lesser degree of reculturing for all those directly affected. Ten or more years later in many contexts, although the use of technology may have become a regular part of school life, the manner in which it is used often remains quite superficial (teachers' notes on PowerPoint for example), and the actual visible teaching and learning practices in many classrooms remain much as they were before its introduction. I believe that it will take a further ten years or more (and ever more sophisticated technology) to reach a point where reculturing has occurred to the extent that the majority of those working with ICT in classrooms understand how it can be used to achieve the 'real' hoped-for changes that will justify its introduction.

Over such long time spans, the environment in which any education system is situated is unlikely to stand still. One common environmental change that frequently affects politically inspired educational-change processes is that the national policy makers with whom the educational change originated are replaced by others, who, for political and/or economic reasons, decide not to retain their predecessors' policies. At worst this can mean abrupt abandonment of (financial and leadership) support for a change initiative and/or the decision to implement it very differently. Such policy shifts seem to occur more often than common sense suggests they should. When they do, of course the human and financial investment that has already been made probably over a number of years is implicitly devalued, and (as in the case in chapter 5) the people affected, especially teachers, may become reluctant to invest their energy in any future changes.

People's experiences affect their behaviour. If policy makers and local leaders wish to introduce changes that will require new behaviours, then their planning needs to try to ensure that people's experiences of change are as positive as possible. For that to be likely, any change needs to be planned bearing people's existing realities in mind. To identify such realities some kind of more or less formal information-gathering exercise ('baseline study') is necessary. Perhaps because carrying out a detailed study at national level would, in most countries, be very complex (and so time consuming and expensive) or perhaps because few governments like to draw explicit attention to the wide variations that exist within their national education system, baseline studies carried out at national level before a change is decided on are rare. Consequently, local educational administrators and institutional change leaders in a wide range of different local contexts may be confronted with the 'requirement' to implement a national change, without the change (or the expected outcomes of the change) having been 'modified' in any way to suit their circumstances. This last section of the book proposes a means of carrying out a simple 'baseline study' at the local/institutional level and shows how the information gathered can be used to inform local implementation planning.

The suggested process centres on two groups of questions, which I believe (Wedell 2003) it is relevant to ask in any educational-change situation. The first group contains questions that aim to identify the current beliefs and skills of all those who will be most directly affected by the proposed change ('People in contexts' in Figure 4.1 on page 48), what degree of reculturing the change represents, and so what support mechanisms will need to be established if the change is to become visible in classrooms.

Societal beliefs about teaching and learning, and hence what is expected of teachers and learners in classrooms, is one influence on how any subject is taught. Another set of influences, which of course overlap to some extent, are the conditions in which the teaching takes place, for example class sizes and available resources, the number of timetable hours available and how the subject is assessed. This second group of questions therefore considers the degree of 'fit' between the existing conditions ('Conditions in contexts' in Figure 4.1) and the conditions that would best support implementation of the proposed changes.

In this section I will use three scenarios as illustrations. They all represent examples of types of educational-change processes that I have personal experience of, and so again relate to language education. However, I believe that the question and answer process I suggest is relevant for educational change in any discipline and of any scale. The scenarios are:

- planning for the implementation of ICT-assisted language learning to support the development of oral/aural skills

- planning for the local implementation of a new national language curriculum whose hoped-for outcomes entail a significant degree of 'reculturing'
- planning the content and process of a new initial language-teacher-education curriculum

For each, I identify a number of questions, under the two main headings above, that I believe that planners in the setting could usefully ask to get a sense of their context before making final planning decisions. I also give one or more possible answers and then discuss what the answer(s) imply for the planning /implementation process. I fully acknowledge that the answers are only examples based on my own experience, and that they will be more or less different in different contexts. However, my purpose for working through the scenarios is to demonstrate how, if change leaders try to obtain answers that are as honest as possible, the information gathered can help guide their decision making in terms of:

- identifying whether/how the proposed change will need to be adjusted to enable implementation to begin in the existing context
- clarifying what support they will need to provide for those who are most affected, before they can expect any classroom implementation to take place
- identifying which groups may continue to need support once implementation has begun, what form such support might take and so how the implementation process should be staged
- sequencing the stages of their planning so that they support and build on each other

Such 'informed' planning should make it more likely that the process is experienced positively by those most directly affected. If this is so, it stands more chance of achieving at least some of the hoped-for (positive) educational outcomes.

For each scenario I provide a brief contextual background and explain the desired outcome of the change proposed. I then consider what questions it would be sensible for local/institutional leaders to ask when they are considering how to implement the change. Finally I offer answers to the questions based on my own experience and, bearing the background in mind, discuss what the information that the answers provide suggests for the planning and/or implementation processes.

Chapter 8

# Introducing ICT to support language teaching in one institution

## 8.1 Background

Institutional leaders at a college with a top-down organizational culture in a country with a broadly transmission-based educational culture are concerned by the poor level of graduates' oral/aural English proficiency after their four years of college study. They decide (without consulting teaching staff) to introduce ICT-assisted learning for three hours a week for each class to try to support the development of students' oral/aural language skills. There are few budgetary constraints. They decide to convert a number of classrooms into computer laboratories, each equipped with a terminal for each member of a single class, and to install examples of up-to-date interactive language-teaching software on each machine. They hope that teachers will use the time in these computer rooms to provide students with regular exposure to a range of different varieties of spoken English and opportunities to practise speaking themselves through one-to-one interaction with the advanced 'chat bot' software that has been installed. The hoped-for outcome is that future learners will graduate with at least basic oral/aural confidence and proficiency. In this scenario there is no practical reason why the leaders should not ask those affected questions directly, although the nature of the organization makes it unlikely to happen. What questions would it then be useful to ask to support implementation planning?

## 8.2 Questions

I mentioned above that I think there are two sets of questions that planners at any level can and should ask when planning any educational change for which they are responsible. The first set of questions revolves around identifying the current understandings, skills, beliefs and behaviours of those who will be most directly affected by the proposed change.

> QUESTIONS TO CONSIDER
> In the scenario outlined above:
> Who might these people be?
> What questions would you want to ask (about) them?

The second set relates to the extent to which existing conditions in which English is taught in the institution (in this case the conditions relating to language teaching, learning and assessment) 'fit' the change and the outcomes it hopes to achieve.

> QUESTIONS TO CONSIDER
> Which conditions might be relevant here?
> What questions would you want to ask about them?

## 8.2.1 Questions about who will be affected

In the above scenario, I think that those most likely to be affected are:

- the teachers
- the learners
- the computer technicians

Some questions it would be useful to ask directly of (or indirectly about) each are given in Table 8.1.

**Table 8.1**   Questions that might be asked of (about) the people most affected by the change.

| Who will be affected | What questions might it be important to ask? |
| --- | --- |
| Teachers | • What teaching methods/approaches do English teachers currently use for developing oral/aural proficiency?<br>• How computer literate are most teachers?<br>• What do answers to these questions suggest about teachers' likely attitude to the proposed change the type and amount of support they will need in order to become able to use the new facilities effectively? |
| Learners | • What is their attitude to learning English? Are they likely to welcome the opportunity to develop oral/aural skills more fully?<br>• Are there any cultural issues that might make them uncomfortable about practising in computer labs?<br>• What level of computer literacy do they already have?<br>• What do answers to these questions suggest about the type and amount of support they will need to become able to use the facilities effectively? |
| Computer technicians | • Do existing technicians have the skills necessary to maintain and provide technical support for the new computer labs?<br>• Is the number of existing technicians sufficient to be able to support the use of the new computer labs/machines?<br>• What do answers to these questions suggest about the need for training or new recruitment? |

## 8.2.2 Questions about conditions influencing how language teaching takes place

Components that I feel are likely to be relevant are:

- the language-teaching curriculum/syllabus, and the teaching and learning principles on which it is based
- the most frequently used learning materials – the textbook
- the format and content of internal and, especially, any external assessments

Again some questions that I feel it would be useful to ask are given below.

**Table 8.2** Questions about the conditions that influence how language teaching takes place in the college.

| Component | Questions it is important to ask |
|---|---|
| Curriculum | • What teaching method/approach is the existing curriculum based on?<br>• How does it view the learning process?<br>• Does it match the teaching–learning approach on which the computer-based learning materials are based?<br>If it does not:<br>• What are the main differences?<br>• What support will need to be provided for whom in order to bridge them? |
| Materials | • What types of oral/aural activity do existing materials offer?<br>• Are they broadly consistent with those offered by the new computer materials?<br>If not:<br>• How will the new software materials need to be introduced?<br>• What aspects of working with them might learners find difficult?<br>• What will teachers need to know and be able to do to make a smooth transition? |
| Assessment | • What aspects of language are currently most frequently assessed and how are they assessed?<br>If oral/aural skills are already assessed:<br>• Will it be necessary to make any changes to the way in which they are assessed?<br>If oral/aural skills are not assessed at present:<br>• Are there plans to begin to test these?<br>• What weighting will they have in the overall 'mark'? |

## 8.3 Answering the questions

Answers to the above questions, especially if they are obtained through direct discussion with representatives of the people involved, can provide institutional leaders with valuable information to guide their implementation planning. Some examples of what I mean can be found in Tables 8.3 and 8.4.

**Table 8.3** Answers to questions about people.

| Questions | Answers |
|---|---|
| What teaching methods/approaches do English teachers currently use for developing oral/aural proficiency? | • They follow a transmission-based curriculum that emphazises the teaching of language knowledge and the development of reading skills. They do no oral/aural practice at all. |
| How computer literate are most teachers? | • Most teachers use computers at home for email and the internet. None have experience of using computers in their teaching. |
| What do the answers to these questions suggest about:how challenging the change will be for teachers? the type and amount of support they will need in order to become able to use the new facilities effectively? | • Teachers are likely to find the proposed change very challenging. • They will need training in: principles of learning and techniques/activities for teaching oral/aural skills technical and classroom-management skills to enable them to use computers for supporting the learning of such skills |
| What attitude do most learners have to learning English? Are they likely to welcome the opportunity to develop oral/aural skills more fully? | • Most learners see knowledge of English as a means of accessing information, films and music and as a gateway to possible overseas study. They are keen to develop oral/aural skills. |
| Are there any cultural issues that might make them uncomfortable about practising in computer labs? | • Because oral/aural skills are poor they become easily embarrassed in front of peers. Computer-based interaction will enable them to begin to practise in a potentially less stressful environment. |
| What level of computer literacy do they already have? | • They are very used to using computers to play games, watch films, listen to music, surf the Web and participate in online networks (in L1). |
| What do the answers to these questions suggest about the type and amount of support they will need to become able to use the facilities effectively? | • They will need little technical assistance. Teachers will need to be able to explain the purpose of learning activities clearly, and be available to help individuals as necessary. |
| Do existing technicians have the skills necessary to maintain and provide technical support for the new computer labs? Is the number of existing technicians sufficient to be able to support the use of the new computer labs/machines? What do answers to these questions suggest about the need for training or new recruitment? | Existing technicians do have the necessary skills. At least one more technician will need to be recruited to ensure that support is available at all times. S/he will need to be able to demonstrate familiarity with the purchased hardware and software. |

The answers in Table 8.3 begin to suggest some of the preparations it will be necessary to make. Those in Table 8.4 provide more useful information.

Table 8.4  Answers to questions about conditions.

| Questions | Answers |
|---|---|
| What teaching method/approach is the existing curriculum based on? | • The existing curriculum is fact based and encourages an idea of teaching as transmission of facts. Teachers lecture and write notes about the language on the board. |
| How does it view the learning process? | • It views learning as memorization of information. |
| Does it match the teaching–learning approach on which the computer-based learning materials are based?<br>If it does not: | • No. The computer-based materials emphasize practice in the use of language for interaction in real time. |
| What are the main differences? | • Moving from a view of language as a set of facts to language as a means of interaction to express/comprehend meanings. |
| What support will need to be provided for whom in order to bridge them? | • Teachers will need training as above. |
| What types of oral/aural activity do the materials offer? | • Linguistically controlled oral drills and very simple scripted role-plays for listening. Teachers do not use them. |
| Are they broadly consistent with those offered by the new computer materials? | • No, they offer no chances for hearing/trying to produce unscripted language in real time. |
| If not: | |
| How will the new materials need to be introduced? | • Through a discussion of the nature of spoken language. |
| What aspects of working with them might learners find difficult? | • The speed and unpredictability of the language, and the acceptance that it is normal to make mistakes when speaking a second language. |
| What will teachers need to know about and be able to do to make a smooth transition? | • They will need to understand and be able to explain the differences between written and spoken language and to provide a rationale for classroom tasks and processes.<br>How to manage oral/aural activities. |
| What aspects of language are currently most frequently tested and how are they tested?<br>If oral/aural skills are not included: | • Grammar, vocabulary and reading comprehension. Tested using multiple-choice questions. |
| Are there plans to begin to test these?<br>What weighting will they have in the overall 'mark'? | • No. |

## 8.4 Establishing what preparations need to be made to support implementation of the change

Tables 8.3 and 8.4 provide institutional planners with an outline of some of the most important preparations that will need to be made if the people who will be affected by the introduction of computer-based language learning are to understand why and how to use it to achieve the hoped-for outcomes.

Teachers will need training in:

- principles of learning and techniques/activities for teaching oral/aural skillsthe use of the new hardware/software for supporting the learning of such skillsclassroom management. They will need to be reminded of differences between written and spoken language and what these imply for their classroom role and response to learner error. They will need to be able to explain the purpose of activities clearly, give clear instructions and understand how it is appropriate to help individuals when necessary.

This will represent a challenge since their previous experience is of teaching based around the accurate transmission of 'correct facts'. They will need to understand how working with learners who are using the computers is different, and to be able to explain this to their learners. They will probably also need to be able to provide a rationale for the difference that will continue to exist between classes using the existing materials, and those using the computer-based materials.

Learners:

- are positively disposed towards the idea of developing their oral/aural skills and most already are quite familiar with the use of computers
- are used to their teachers taking full responsibility for all learning in the classroom. Their experience is principally of language learning as memorization. They are used to being judged on the accuracy of any answers they give
- will therefore need explicit explanation of how the computer-based classes will be different from their existing classes: what they will be expected to do; what the purpose of doing it is; what to do if they do not understand; what to do if they make mistakes

Technicians:

- Existing technicians will need to familiarize themselves with the new hard- and software.
- Another appropriately experienced/qualified technician will need to be employed.
- Technicians will need time to consider what basic technical information and skills teachers will need in order to be able to manage classes effectively, and how best to enable them to acquire these.

### 8.4.1 Curriculum and materials

There are no plans to change these. Learners will continue to spend the bulk of their language-learning time in the learning environment that they are familiar with. It will be necessary for teachers to be able to explain what each type of learning is trying to achieve. In the medium term it may be necessary to reconsider the mismatch between the two different learning environments.

### 8.4.2 Assessment of oral/aural ability

This is currently not assessed in any way and the original plans for change did not include any intention to develop assessment in this area. Institutional leaders need to consider the implications of not assessing such performance.

- What effect may it have on the seriousness with which teachers and learners take the computer-based learning?
- What effect may a lack of seriousness have on the likelihood of achieving the hoped-for outcomes of the change?

## 8.5 Deciding on an order in which to make the preparations

> QUESTION TO CONSIDER
> If you were responsible for making the above preparations, what would your priorities be? In what order would you plan what needed to be done?

Those most centrally affected and most likely to be challenged by the proposed change are the teachers. I would therefore begin by considering how to provide the training they need to be able to begin implementation. I have seen that they need training in both professional and technical skills; so training will need to include:

1. discussion of how written and spoken language differ
2. discussion of the learning conditions that are likely to support the development of oral/aural skills
3. discussion of how to explain the respective language-learning purposes of the very different computer- and existing materials-based classes
4. discussion of/practice in how to explain (1)–(3) to the learners
5. information about, and practice in, the technical aspects of running a class in the computer labs
6. an introduction to, and opportunities to become familiar with, the techniques and activities that the software uses to provide practice in the development of such skills
7. discussion of/practice in new classroom-management skills and the giving of clear instructions for new types of learner activity

8. discussion of/practice in new aspects of their role as teachers when supporting students in the use of the software. Important here will be the development of noticing skills, to be able to judge when and how to intervene.

As is obvious, most aspects of such training involve more than merely communicating factual information. They also involve adjusting their teacherly roles and developing new skills. As seen in chapter 7.2 in the previous section, such learning cannot be accomplished in a matter of hours or days. Teachers are likely to need a series of training sessions over several months, interspersed between experiences of 'trying out' classroom implementation. Designing training provision in this way would mean that when teachers encountered implementation problems they would know that there will be an opportunity to share these and seek advice from someone more 'expert' at the next training session. This hopefully makes it less likely that they will feel discouraged and demotivated by the inevitable early difficulties.

A first stage of planning for implementation might therefore be to:

- agree the content and time needed for teachers' technical training with the technicians
- identify an appropriate professional trainer and discuss the length and design of the training provision. Issues to be discussed here include what aspects of the training it will be essential to provide before implementation begins, how many further cycles of training will be needed during the early implementation stages and at what stage the purely technical training should be provided.
- book appropriate training provision for agreed dates
- consider what systems might be established to encourage teachers to help each other during initial implementation stages in between the more formal training
- decide on any timetable adjustments needed during the early implementation stages to accommodate the above training and to provide time for teachers to meet to share problems and solutions

A second stage that would need to happen more or less simultaneously with the above would be to:

- recruit an appropriately experienced technician
- provide time for all technicians to familiarize themselves with the new hardware/software and to prepare a technical training programme for the teachers

A third stage, again probably needing to happen more or less in parallel with (or very shortly after) the others, would be:

- to consider the importance of giving 'weight' to the work done in computer-based classes by formally assessing it in some way

If a decision is made to do so, further training in developing performance-based assessment will be necessary for at least some teachers.

## 8.6 Conclusion

I am sure that you can probably think of other questions it would be appropriate to ask, and of course in your context there would be different answers to at least some of the questions. What I have tried to do here is show that, by using two sets of simple questions that can be asked of *any* change context, it is possible to obtain information that can guide the implementation-planning process in important ways. It will not mean that implementation will be problem free, but it does mean that some of the main problems that might arise will have already been thought about – and hopefully planned for. This should make them easier to cope with, and so mean they have fewer negative effects on implementers.

In this chapter I have looked at a single change in a single institution. In the next I try to apply the same sets of questions to local implementation of a national change.

# Chapter 9

# Introducing a new national curriculum

## 9.1 Background

Over the past decades, one frequent example of educational change worldwide has been the move by more and more national governments to make proficiency in English a central pillar of their education strategy (Graddol 2006). An example of this trend can be seen in Japan. Here the 2002 plan to cultivate 'Japanese with English Abilities' states:

> With the progress of globalization in the economy and in society, it is essential that our children acquire communication skills in English, which has become a common international language, in order for living in the 21st century. This has become an extremely important issue both in terms of the future of our children and the further development of Japan as a nation. (Ministry of Education, Tokyo, 12 July 2002)

Broadly similar rationales, based around the need to try to enable *children to acquire communication skills in English* in order to maintain national competitiveness in an ever more global market, have led educational policy makers in many countries to decide on some or all of the following:

- to change the content and weighting of state-school curricula to emphasize the development of communication skills
- to introduce English as a core subject earlier in the curriculum
- to make success in national high-stakes English examinations an essential determinant of ultimate educational and/or occupational achievement

The background to the change in this chapter is a decision by policy makers in a centralized education system to introduce a new national English curriculum to the state-secondary-education system. The stated purpose of doing so is to enable the majority of learners to leave school with at least a basic level of oral and written communication skills in English. It is hoped that, in an international context in which English is currently the dominant language, this change will benefit both citizens and the nation. A set of new national textbooks, specifically designed to help teachers and learners achieve the hoped-for outcomes of the change, have been developed. It has been planned that copies of these will be available in all schools by the time implementation begins.

The assumptions commonly held about the purposes and processes of education, and the way in which the education system and the institutions within it should be organized, remain towards the left ends of the continua presented in Figures 3.1 and 3.2. The content and sequence of the new curriculum has borrowed extensively from similar curricula elsewhere in the world. Its emphasis on the development of learners' language skills represents a shift from a long-standing tendency to view learning English as just another school subject whose content is a well-defined set of knowledge about English grammar, vocabulary, spelling, etc. that needs to be memorized. For this shift in focus to become visible in most classrooms, some existing assumptions about teaching and learning will have to change greatly.

National policy makers decided on the change without direct consultation with representatives of those whom it would affect. However, prior to implementation of the curriculum, educational administrators at all levels were required to attend regional briefings designed to explain the reasons for the change and its hoped-for outcomes as outlined above, and to provide information about the funding available for its implementation. They are responsible for planning, managing and monitoring implementation in their own areas.

In what follows I am assuming (and this may often be an inaccurate assumption) that as a result of the above briefings, local educational leaders begin their implementation planning with at least a broad understanding of why the change matters, what it hopes to achieve, how it hopes to achieve it and how much time and money they have to begin the implementation process in their area. Of course, as previously mentioned, the exact route and rate of the implementation process will vary from one area (and probably from one school) to another. Local leaders therefore need to develop an implementation plan that will be suitable for the schools in their area. To help inform this process I again see the two sets of questions introduced in chapter 8 as the starting point.

## 9.2 Questions

The first set of questions again tries to help identify the current understandings, skills, beliefs and behaviours of those who will be most directly affected by the proposed change.

> QUESTION TO CONSIDER
> Who might these people be in any local educational environment?
> What questions would you want to ask (about) them?

The next set relates to the extent to which existing classroom conditions within local institutions (in this case conditions that affect teaching, learning and assessment generally, and the teaching, learning and assessment of English in particular) are appropriate for the outcomes that the change hopes to achieve.

---

QUESTION TO CONSIDER
Which of the existing conditions that influence the existing educational (English teaching) system are likely to be relevant here?
What questions would you want to ask about them?

---

## 9.2.1 Questions about who will be affected

A range of people are likely to be more or less directly affected by, and also affect, the successful implementation of the curriculum change. Those most likely to be directly affected are listed below:

- English teachers whose existing, and probably deeply held, professional assumptions about what makes them a 'good teacher' will be challenged by the new curriculum, and will need support to develop new skills and understandings
- teacher educators who will be responsible for helping teachers develop such new understandings and skills
- learners whose assumptions about what is expected of them may no longer be appropriate for English classes that are trying to develop their language skills
- institutional leaders whose assumptions about what appropriate teaching and learning behaviours are like will need to change if they are to provide the active support that English teachers will need during the early implementation stage
- if a separate group of inspectors or supervisors responsible for evaluating teachers' performance exists within the system, they will need to understand what the curriculum change implies for the concept of good teaching, and adapt their evaluation criteria accordingly

Less directly affected may be:

- teachers of other subjects, whose curricula have not been changed; these may not understand the changes their English-teaching colleagues are being asked to make, and/or may not view them positively
- parents whose expectations of 'proper' education and 'good' teaching are based around seeing tangible evidence of the 'knowledge' their children have learned; they may be upset if such evidence is no longer fully available for all English lessons

Some questions that I feel that local-change leaders could usefully ask about each group of people are given in Table 9.1.

**Table 9.1**   Questions that might be asked of (about) the people most affected by the change.

| Who will be affected? | What questions might it be important to ask? |
|---|---|
| Local teachers | • What are the essential skills and understandings that the new curriculum requires of English teachers?<br>• What are their current professional strengths and weaknesses?<br>• What are the most important gaps between their current strengths and what the new curriculum expects?<br>• What do these gaps suggest about priorities? Are there areas in which they will definitely need support before implementation begins? What will be needed during the early stages of implementation?<br>• What do these gaps suggest about the time needed to prepare for implementation? |
| Local teacher educators | • Given the most important gaps identified above, do local teacher educators have the knowledge, understanding and skills to provide appropriate support? |
| Learners | • What changes in classroom behaviour will be needed if learners are to benefit from the new curriculum?<br>• How can learners be helped to understand these and why they are important? |
| Institutional leaders | • How do they view good teaching?<br>• What do they know about the proposed change?<br>• Do they understand its implications for classroom practice?<br>• What is their role in supporting the implementation process?<br>• What information/support will help them play a positive role? |
| Inspectors/supervisors (if they exist) | • How do they currently evaluate teachers and teaching? Is this consistent with the aims of the curriculum change?<br>• Do they need training to adjust their evaluation criteria? Who should provide this? |
| Teachers of other subjects? | • Since they will not be facing similar changes, how can they be encouraged to support their English-teaching colleagues? |
| Parents | • How can they be helped to understand the changes in what will be expected of their children in English classes? |

The very process of identifying questions such as those above can in itself raise local leaders' awareness of some of the issues that they will probably have to address in their implementation planning. The issues already mentioned become a little clearer, and further issues are added, by the second set of questions.

## 9.2.2 Questions about the existing conditions that influence the education and language-teaching systems

The wider education system, and components of the language-education system, will also affect the planning and implementation of the change, since they will inevitably influence the existing expectations and behaviours of all the groups of people discussed above.

Within the education system as a whole, the following are likely to be relevant:

- the existing 'educational culture' (see chapter 3.2) will strongly affect both how those working in various capacities within education, and how those affected by education in society at large, view the purpose, content and process of education. This 'culture' will include assumptions about teacher and learner behaviour, the conditions needed for effective learning to occur and how learning can be assessed. Such assumptions develop over time in every society as a result of complex combinations of social, political, religious and economic influences and experiences, and are frequently extremely deeply rooted. The more reculturing of people that a change requires in order to meet its aims, the more complicated the implementation process will be and the longer it is likely to take

The educational culture is likely to be reflected in:

- the national assessment system: the accepted format and content of high-stakes exams – such as (in many countries) the university-entrance test and the degree of collaboration between national-education policy makers and those responsible for the design and administration of such important exams
- the teacher-education system: the content and process of initial teacher education. The national system for in-service teacher development (if it exists)

Within the language-education system, the ease with which it is possible to implement a new curriculum will be influenced by:

- whether teaching conditions in most classrooms are supportive of the kinds of classroom roles and activities that the new curriculum hopes to introduce. Factors likely to be relevant include:
  - the number of learners in most classrooms
  - learners' attitude and motivation for learning English
  - the number of English classes each week
  - the time within the working week that teachers have for preparation
  - the degree to which teachers are used to making their own decisions about how to approach teaching in different classes
  - whether teachers and learners have access to enough suitable teaching materials

- the socio-economic status of English teachers and so their likely willingness to spend time and energy on any necessary 'reculturing'
- the specific demands of the English-assessment system for learners at different levels

Questions that local leaders might need to ask about existing reality in most schools in their own area are suggested in Table 9.2.

**Table 9.2**　Questions about the conditions that influence how language teaching takes place in schools.

| Condition | Questions |
|---|---|
| Educational culture | • How are teachers and learners conventionally expected to behave in the classroom? <br>• How is learning thought to take place? <br>• How is learning normally assessed? <br>• What important differences exist between answers to the above questions and the behaviours and ideas about learning and assessment that the new curriculum hopes to introduce? <br>• What do these differences suggest that learners and their parents need to understand about the changes? <br>• What do these differences suggest for the design and content of support that teachers will need? <br>• Are there sufficient (any?) local teacher educators who understand how to design and provide effective support for teachers? <br>• What do answers to the above suggest about how long local leaders will need to actively manage the implementation process? |
| The national-assessment system | • Are the content and format of national high-stakes tests going to change to match the hoped-for outcomes of the new curriculum? |
| The teacher-training system | • Are there plans to change the national initial teacher-education curriculum for English teachers to develop the understandings and skills that the new curriculum expects new teachers to have? Do these have local implications? <br>• Is there an existing local in-service teacher-development system? <br>• Does its structure easily lend itself to the type of support that will need to be provided for existing teachers? |
| Classroom conditions | • How many learners are there in most English classrooms? <br>• Do most learners and their parents view learning English positively? <br>• How many hours per week of English do learners have? <br>• Do teachers have time during working hours to prepare for their classes? <br>• Are teachers used to making their own decisions about what and how to teach? <br>• Will the above conditions support teachers trying to implement the sort of teaching that the new curriculum expects? |
| Teaching materials | • By the time implementation starts, will there be enough appropriate teaching materials in most classrooms? |

| Teachers' socio-economic status | • Are English teachers generally satisfied with their jobs? <br> • Can they live adequately on their salaries without having to do further private work? <br> • Can teachers reasonably be expected to spend the extra time that implementation will demand, without further reward? |
|---|---|
| Assessment of English | • What are the most important English exams that learners have to take? <br> • When do they occur? <br> • What do they assess? <br> • Are there any ways in which the demands of assessment may affect teachers' and learners' willingness to work using the new curriculum? |

## 9.3 Answering the questions

How local leaders set about answering the questions will of course vary considerably. Few are likely to be fully trained evaluators and researchers, and in many contexts there will be pressure from national policy makers to move towards implementation as rapidly as possible. In such circumstances there will be neither the specialist skills nor the time to carry out a full baseline study in which answers to complex questions like those above are systematically sought, and their answers analysed and considered before plans for implementation are made. More often answers may only be partial, based on local leaders' experience of their local context and (hopefully) discussion with at least some English-teacher educators, institutional leaders and members of their staff.

The accuracy of data gathered in such an informal manner may be questioned. Reluctance to admit that there are problems with existing provision, prior experience of negative responses to honest appraisals from those higher up the educational hierarchy, or genuine lack of understanding of what is being asked, may all make people reluctant and/or unable to provide an honest assessment of their existing realities. Local leaders can set an example in their own attitude to the question–answer process, but ultimately carrying out the process suggested here will only be worthwhile if the information gathered provides a more or less honest reflection of the local reality. Where it does so, regardless of its strict 'reliability' in research terms, the information gathered can help local planners to develop a clearer picture of some of the main issues they will need to consider in their implementation planning. I try to illustrate this in Tables 9.3 and 9.4 below.

Table 9.3 further highlights aspects of the local reality that local leaders will need to consider in their plans. It begins to give a sense of implementation as an ongoing process in which teachers especially, but also learners and institutional leaders, will need support over time. Table 9.4 helps develop the picture further.

Answers in Table 9.4 explain the context into which the change is being introduced further, and help raise awareness of some of the most significant 'gaps' that will need to be worked on if the hoped-for outcomes of the new curriculum are to become visible in the local classroom reality. The next section summarizes

**Table 9.3** Some answers to questions about the people who will be affected.

| Questions | Answers |
|---|---|
| **Local teachers**<br>What are the essential skills and understandings that the new curriculum requires of English teachers? | • Good personal-language skills.<br>• A good understanding of the structure of English and its vocabulary. Understanding of ideas about how people learn to use languages, and knowledge about and confidence in using classroom techniques that will help learners develop communication skills. |
| What are their current professional strengths and weaknesses?<br>What are the most important gaps between their current strengths and what the new curriculum expects? | • Variable personal-language proficiency.<br>• Good teachers of grammar and vocabulary.<br>• Teachers' variable language proficiency.<br>• Little knowledge of current ideas about foreign-language learning and no experience of teaching language skills.<br>• Limited range of classroom-management skills. |
| What do these gaps suggest about priorities? Are there areas in which they will definitely need support before implementation begins/what will be needed during the early stages of implementation? | *Before implementation:*<br>• Teachers' language proficiency is a priority if they are to feel confident enough to develop new teaching approaches.<br>• An introduction to ideas about how language skills are learned.<br>• Chances to experience and try out some basic skill-development techniques used in the new textbooks.<br><br>*During implementation:*<br>• Ongoing language and methodological support during the first few years of the implementation.<br>• Periods of formal training will ideally be followed by linked practice time in school, supported by more 'expert' mentors. |
| What do these gaps suggest about the time needed to prepare for implementation? | • If teachers are to be properly prepared, implementation should not begin for at least a year or two. |
| **Teacher educators**<br>Given the most important gaps identified above, do local teacher educators have the knowledge, understanding and skills to provide appropriate support? | • They can help develop teachers' language proficiency.<br>• Most are familiar with current ideas about learning to use a foreign language |

| | |
|---|---|
| | and the teaching approaches recommended to try to enable such learning to take place. |
| | • They have little experience of using ideas in practice, so may need training in demonstrating teaching approaches. |
| | • They know little about current views of teacher learning and what these imply for the design, content and process of training course design. |
| **Learners**<br>What changes in classroom behaviour will be needed if learners are to benefit from the new curriculum? | • They will no longer find that taking notes of what the teacher writes on the board and memorizing these is sufficient to do well in English. |
| | • They will be expected to participate in skill-development activities, sometimes with others. These will often involve making personal choices about language |
| How can learners be helped to understand these changes and why they are important? | use, which will sometimes be 'incorrect'. |
| | • Changes in expectation, and the reasons behind them, need to be explained simply, and probably repeatedly, by institutional leaders and teachers, during the first months of implementation. |
| **Institutional leaders**<br>How do they view good teaching?<br>What do they know about the proposed change? | • See educational culture below.<br>• They have been officially told that the new curriculum will be introduced, but have had no further information. |
| Do they understand its implications for classroom practice? | • No. |
| What is their role in supporting the implementation process? | • Given the support that teachers will need before and during the implementation stage, they will need to be flexible in terms of providing time and space for more or less formal training. |
| What information/support will help them play a positive role? | • Local leaders will need to brief them about the rationale for the changes and their role over time in supporting their teachers' implementation efforts. |
| **Inspectors/supervisors**<br>How do they currently evaluate teachers and teaching? | • There are no inspectors in this context. Teachers are evaluated within their schools mostly according to their learners' exam results. |
| Is this consistent with the aims of the curriculum change?<br>Do they need training to adjust their evaluation criteria?<br>Who should provide this? | |

| Colleagues teaching other subjects<br>Since they will not be facing similar changes, how can they be encouraged to support their English-teaching colleagues? | • Institutional leaders will need to provide some basic information about/ rationale for the changes and encourage everyone to support those involved in them. |
|---|---|
| Parents<br>How can they be helped to understand the changes in what will be expected of their children in English classes? | • Local leaders will need to decide on awareness-raising/information sharing strategies to explain simply why and how the work their children do in English classes is to change. |

the implication of some answers in Tables 9.3 and 9.4 for the local planning of change implementation.

## 9.4 Establishing what preparations need to be made to support change implementation

Successfully planning and managing implementation of a national change at a local level, where the professional strengths and weaknesses of different institutions and the personal feelings/reactions of a large number of people all potentially influence planning outcomes, is an enormous challenge. Results of implementation planning will depend on the degree to which such local planning is informed by a more detailed awareness of the many interrelated contextual variables than it is possible to introduce in this example. However, although the information in Tables 9.3 and 9.4 is only illustrative and partial, I believe that there is great value in thinking through what it can tell planners about the sorts of practical implementation decisions they will have to make. Here I make the big assumption that, thanks to the national briefings they have attended and their high level of professionalism, local planners do fully understand the important aspects of the change, and are therefore able to use the information that they have gathered effectively.

> QUESTION TO CONSIDER
> How might the information in Tables 9.3 and 9.4 above help inform your planning of the following aspects of the change-implementation process?
>     communicating the change appropriately to those affected by it
>     preparing/supporting teachers to begin implementation

The central figures whose attitudes and behaviours will determine the success of this, or any other, educational change are of course the classroom English teachers, and I therefore begin by discussing preparation relating to these. But, as is obvious from the tables, the manner in which, and the enthusiasm with which, teachers

**Table 9.4** Some answers to questions about the conditions that influence the general education and English-language-teaching systems.

| Questions | Answers |
|---|---|
| **Educational culture** | |
| How are teachers and learners conventionally expected to behave in the classroom? | ● Teacher–learner relationships are formal. Teachers talk and learners listen and take notes. Learners rarely speak apart from asking or answering questions. |
| How is learning thought to take place? | ● Largely through memorization of factual information. |
| How is learning normally assessed? | ● Usually through exams that test accurate recall of factual information. |
| What important differences exist between answers to the above questions and the behaviours and ideas about learning and assessment that the new curriculum hopes to introduce? | ● Depending on the focus of each stage of the lesson, the curriculum assumptions include: less rigid classroom relationships greater participation by learners greater variety of classroom activity more English spoken in class assessment of performance as well as knowledge |
| What do these differences suggest that learners and their parents need to understand about the changes? | ● Learners and their parents will need to be helped to understand the reasons for, and value of, the changes. |
| What do these differences suggest for the design and content of support that teachers will need? | ● Teachers will need to make great professional adjustments to their thinking and behaviour. They will need opportunities to recognize the above differences, to discuss how they might be introduced in their classrooms, and to experience them and practise them over time. |
| Are there sufficient local teacher educators who understand how to design and provide effective support for teachers? | ● Educators share most aspects of the educational culture with teachers. They will probably need some training before they begin to work with teachers. |
| What do answers to the above suggest about the length of time during which local leaders will need to actively manage the implementation process? | ● Several years at least. Planners need to think about staging the process. |
| **High-stakes assessment** | |
| Are the content and format of national high stakes English tests going to change to match the hoped-for outcomes of the new curriculum? | ● There is no intention to change high stakes tests at this stage. They continue to reflect the existing knowledge-based curriculum. |
| **Existing teacher-education provision** | |
| Are there plans to change the national initial teacher-education curriculum for English teachers to develop the understandings and skills that the new curriculum expects new teachers to have? Do these have local implications? | ● Local planners are not responsible for initial teacher education. |
| Is there an existing local in-service teacher-development system? Does its structure easily lend itself to the type of support that will need to be provided for existing teachers? | ● The existing in-service training system provides short (maximum one week) formal courses outside school. These aim to provide teachers with new professional information |

| | |
|---|---|
| | through lectures and/or the viewing and discussion of model lessons. |
| | ● The design, content, process and duration of courses to support curriculum change will need to be reconsidered. |
| **Classroom conditions**<br>How many learners are there in most English classrooms?<br>Do most learners and their parents view learning English positively?<br>How many hours per week of English do learners have?<br>Do teachers have time during working hours to prepare for their classes?<br>Are teachers used to making their own decisions about what and how to teach?<br><br>Will the above conditions support teachers trying to implement the sort of teaching that the new curriculum expects? | ● Numbers range from 45 to 70.<br>● A minority are very positive, the remainder are indifferent.<br>● 4–6 hours per week throughout secondary school.<br>● Little scheduled time is available.<br><br>● Most teachers are used to 'following the book' closely, although they may decide to skip parts of it.<br>● Conditions will make it difficult to implement the curriculum as ideally intended. Teachers, teacher educators and institutional leaders will need to discuss how to adjust the initial stages of implementation before any training sessions are offered. |
| **Teaching materials**<br>By the time implementation starts, will there be enough appropriate teaching materials in most classrooms? | ● National policy makers have said the new textbooks will be available by the time implementation begins. They need to be available for teachers before this, since working with the new textbooks will be an important part of their training. |
| **English teachers' socio-economic situation**<br>Are English teachers generally satisfied with their jobs?<br>Can they live adequately on their salaries without having to do further private work?<br>Can teachers reasonably be expected to spend the extra time that implementation will demand, without further reward? | ● Yes.<br><br>● Most teachers feel they need to augment their salaries with private work.<br>● If no tangible rewards are offered, the time needed for training needs to be made available within the working day/week. |
| **English exams**<br>What are the most important English exams learners have to take?<br>When do they occur?<br>What do they assess?<br><br><br>Are there any ways in which the demands of assessment may affect teachers' and learners' willingness to work using the new curriculum? | ● English exams matter greatly for entry to good secondary schools and universities.<br>● The final year of school.<br>● They generally assess knowledge about the language and reading and very simple writing only. There has been no official statement that this will change.<br>● Teachers at lower levels are more likely to base their teaching around the curriculum than those at higher levels nearer to the exam. |

anywhere will approach the implementation of a complex change will be strongly influenced by the behaviour of many other people and the extent to which they can see that relevant external factors have been taken into account. Professional support for teachers is very important, but so is the provision of a supportive atmosphere in the implementation environment.

### 9.4.1 Teachers

Preparing the English teachers to implement the new curriculum cannot be a simple matter of telling them about what they are supposed to do and then leaving them to get on with it. The tables show that there are substantial gaps between teachers' current professional strengths and those that they will need to develop in order to implement the new curriculum effectively. To bridge these gaps they will need support both before and during the implementation. Preparations for implementation will therefore need to decide on how to deal with matters such as the following.

#### 9.4.1.1 Communicating the change to teachers

Local English teachers have so far had little or no direct information about the new curriculum, although of course rumours are circulating. Ideally, all teachers should receive similar messages about the new curriculum and what it implies for them. Local planners thus need to decide on issues like:

- what exactly do they need to know? Is the aim just to inform them or also to answer questions that they may have?
- when and how are teachers going to be told about the change? Should they be told only when preparations for training are complete or before?
- who should provide the information, their institutional leaders or the local educational planners? This decision will determine whether they are briefed in their schools or brought together elsewhere in one or more groups.

#### 9.4.1.2 Providing professional support for teachers

The tables show that teachers will need considerable training and support to become able to implement the curriculum (suitably adapted for local circumstances – see below) more or less as intended. National policy makers will almost certainly have set a deadline for implementation to begin. There will need to be some sort of initial, pre-implementation training to enable the deadline to be met. However, given the 'reculturing' that will be needed for teachers to become able to teach the new curriculum, other training needs are certain to emerge during the early stages of the implementation process. An important aspect of preparation is therefore to decide on which aspects of the new knowledge, skills and experiences such pre-implementation training should focus on, and which can be left to be worked on over the first months or years of the actual implementation process itself.

### 9.4.1.3 *Training before implementation begins*

Issues that will need to be decided on here include:

- the key content and aims of the pre-implementation training. These will be influenced by a range of other factors (see 9.4.2–9.4.8 below)
- how long the pre-training needs to be to enable trainers to have time to deal properly with all the essential issues
- how the training should be designed to provide an appropriate balance between confidence building, input, discussion, experiencing new approaches and techniques, trying them out, etc. (see Malderez and Wedell, 2007 in chapters 5–7 for more detailed information)
- whether this training should include language development for teachers whose proficiency is poor, or whether this should be provided separately (or not at all)
- whether all teachers should be trained directly or whether a cascade model of training should be adopted, in which some teachers from each institution or district within the area are trained and they are then expected to pass the content of the training on to their colleagues. Since the training is not just a matter of passing on information, if a cascade model is decided on, those expected to 'cascade' would need additional time to prepare for their role.

### 9.4.1.4 *Training during the early stages of implementation*

Some similar and some different issues will need to be addressed, including:

- what the focus of such training should be and how it will be linked to what has been provided above (again, issues at 9.4.2–9.4.8 will influence decisions here)
- where and how often it should take place
- how long funding will be available to allow training to be facilitated/ organized by external experts (teacher educators) before each school is expected to develop its own support systems
- what preparations institutional leaders will need to be encouraged to make to enable training to take place as planned
- whether it is in fact possible to plan the content of such support in detail at this stage or whether it would be better to postpone detailed planning of content until implementation has begun and the areas in which teachers need further support become clearer. If this decision is taken, it will be particularly important to develop simple monitoring systems to help identify such areas once they begin to emerge.

### 9.4.1.5 *Providing a supportive environment for teachers*

Providing practical professional support to enable English teachers to develop new skills and understandings is essential. It is also important to remember that teachers (like people everywhere) are more likely to continue to be motivated to try to implement change if they can see that what they are being asked to do is realistically achievable in their circumstances (see 9.4.6) and is recognized and appreciated by those around them. Ideally therefore, preparation for implementation would also include consideration both of classroom realities and of how the educational (colleagues, institutional leaders, and the local planners themselves) and wider environments (parents especially) can be encouraged to show their support for the change, or at least minimize any disparaging comments or negative behaviours.

## 9.4.2 Teacher educators

In an ideal situation, discussion of all issues relating to supporting teachers would involve the majority of local teacher educators. Here Tables 9.3 and 9.4 suggest that, given the prevailing tendency to view teaching and learning as principally involving the transmission of knowledge, local teacher educators will probably be more comfortable, competent and confident telling teachers about theories and new approaches and techniques than enabling teachers to experience and practise these. In addition, few teacher educators are likely to be familiar with the training principles underlying the design and facilitation of the practical teacher-development courses that English teachers will need during both types of training outlined above.

They would therefore benefit from a trainer-training course that focuses on:

- skills needed to plan and design practically oriented teacher-development courses
- training and facilitation skills that will enable them to help teachers to, for example:
  - 'see' the differences between their present practices and those expected by the new curriculum
  - discuss, bearing their classroom conditions in mind, which aspects of the change as embodied in the new textbooks it would be most feasible to begin implementing
  - experience and practise whichever aspects are agreed upon

Whether such a trainer-training course can be provided of course depends on:

- how much time there is before implementation is supposed to begin
- funding
- whether appropriate trainer trainers are available locally, regionally or nationally
- whether local teacher educators themselves recognize the need and would therefore participate in such a course positively

If trainer training is not possible, plans for pre- and during-implementation teacher-support provision will need to be based around utilizing the most relevant areas of teacher educators' existing strengths. What form implementation takes, and the expected outcomes, will need to be adjusted accordingly.

### 9.4.3 Institutional leaders

The heads of the schools in which the change is to be implemented are the people in authority with whom teachers most frequently come into contact. They are the people who through their leadership can strongly influence the extent to which the school 'positively welcomes' the change, and so the 'moral support' felt by teachers who are trying to implement it. They can make it more or less easy for teachers to participate in whatever during-implementation training is provided. Since their positive attitude and behaviour is so important, they need to fully understand and support the change.

As part of their preparation, planners will therefore need to consider issues such as:

- what information about the curriculum change itself, and their role in supporting it, institutional leaders need to be provided with
- in what form such information should be provided and who should be responsible for providing it
- what information about funding each institution will need to have, and how directive planners ought to be (can be) about how they expect the money to be spent
- whether it will be necessary to be explicit about institutional leaders' responsibility for creating and maintaining a positive orientation towards working towards the hoped-for outcomes of the change, and how this can best be expressed
- how to make it as easy as possible for institutional leaders to release teachers for training before and during implementation, especially since, if teachers are to feel encouraged and appreciated, the bulk of such training should take place during working hours.

### 9.4.4 Learners

It is rare for learners to be explicitly considered when preparing for change implementation. They, together with teachers, are those who will be most directly affected by the introduction of the new curriculum. In addition, their cooperation and willingness to participate when implementation begins will seriously affect how teachers experience the process, and learners' satisfaction with their experiences of the new curriculum will often be passed on to parents (see below). It seems wise therefore to give some consideration to learners at the planning stage and some issues planners might think about here include:

- how the curriculum change will affect the learners most obviously

- how the changes in what is expected of them, and the benefits that it is hoped that they will bring, can best be explained to them
- whether it might be wise to have 'how to explain the new curriculum to the learners' as one important discussion topic for all teachers during their pre-implementation training

## 9.4.5 Parents

Given the strong competition that increasingly characterizes education in many contexts, and the role that educational success is felt to have in determining children's future prospects, parents' attitudes to a change process (as a result, for example, of their children's responses, or their worries about how it will affect their children's exams prospects) can have a strong positive or negative influence on schools and teachers. Consequently it would be wise for planners to consider:

- how, given parents' (albeit probably unconscious) membership of the existing educational culture, they can most effectively be introduced to the purpose of the changes, the implications for teaching and learning and the hoped-for positive outcomes
- whether there is any tangible evidence in the local, regional, national, international context that could be used to support the claim that the new curriculum will lead to better outcomes

## 9.4.6 Actual classroom conditions

Table 9.4 suggests that local classroom conditions are not ideal for achievement of the hoped-for curriculum outcomes. Local planners are unlikely to be able to change these conditions in any meaningful way before implementation begins. Plans to begin implementation therefore need to bear them in mind. Decisions about the content and structure of both pre- and during-implementation training will need to consider the fact that teachers will be working in what I would consider to be 'large classes', with learners whose motivation varies, and with little time during working hours to prepare classes. During the pre-implementation training, teachers will need to be given time to discuss these realities further and, with teacher educators, explore how they may influence initial implementation of the new curriculum. Plans for ongoing training/support during implementation will hopefully mean that over time teachers in all schools will be able to work out how to implement the new curriculum more fully.

## 9.4.7 Teaching materials

Planners need to try and arrange for these (especially the 'Teacher Books' if they exist) to be available well before implementation is expected to start. Teachers, and teacher educators in particular, need the chance to familiarize themselves with the information and guidance about new teaching approaches and techniques and how lessons using the new curriculum are supposed to be organised. The materials are a physical manifestation of the new curriculum. They will provide a means for teachers and their trainers on the pre-implementation training courses to see what is expected to happen in classrooms, and to agree about the best ways in which to begin the implementation process in local schools. They also represent an important training resource, enabling teacher educators to demonstrate new teaching approaches and activities, and teachers to practise using them themselves.

## 9.4.8 Assessment

Local planners are likely to be only too aware that (as in most parts of the world) institutional leaders, learners and their parents view exam success as the most important measure of the success of secondary education. High-stakes exams exert many more or less direct influences over what happens in school classrooms and on how those within and outside the education system evaluate the performance of schools and their teachers and learners.

National policy makers have not as yet planned to redesign the format and content of such exams to begin to assess the language performance, which is the hoped-for outcome of the new curriculum, as well as (or eventually instead of) language knowledge. Consequently, it is almost certain that teachers' and learners' enthusiasm for working with the new curriculum will decline as the final year of secondary school – the examination year – draws closer.

Bearing this in mind, especially if funds are limited, local planners may feel that their preparations for implementation should focus on the early years of secondary education during which such exam pressure is least strong. They may also feel that it is important to develop local-assessment systems that try to explicitly support the intentions of the curriculum during the first few years of secondary school, by acknowledging that assessment of learners' performance is at least as important as assessment of their knowledge about the language. If this is a priority, then developing local teachers' capacities to assess their learners' performance in a reasonably valid and reliable manner will become an important focus for training.

## 9.4.9 Summary

The discussion above shows that preparing for local-change implementation in a manner that tries to bear in mind the main features of the existing change context is complex and messy. Decisions about one aspect of the planning, for example ensuring that teachers are prepared, may be constrained by the need to bear in mind a range of other issues – for example classroom conditions and what degree of support teacher educators can in fact provide. Local leaders' ability to fully implement a change may be limited by the influence of national issues like high-stakes tests that actually make implementation more difficult. Funding, and how to spend it to best effect, is almost always an issue. In addition, given the length of time that any 'reculturing' can take, there are always questions to be asked about how feasible it really is to plan ahead in great detail, when the issues that actual implementation gives rise to, and the needs of the individuals involved, are themselves likely to be change over time. The next section tries to sequence some of the issues that I have mentioned here.

## 9.5 Deciding on an order in which to make the preparations

As in chapter 8, when it comes to deciding a sequence of events the first focus is on the central figures in any change process: the teachers. Section 9.4 suggested that providing teachers with the support needed to implement the change as fully as local circumstances allow would be a two-stage process. It would begin with a first stage that tried to equip them with a basic understanding of the changes, and with techniques that would allow them to begin some form of implementation. Their skills and understandings would then hopefully develop further through ongoing classroom practice and training during the first stages of actual implementation. Given that there is almost certain to be time pressure in the form of central government guidelines (if not deadlines) about when implementation should begin, one sensible sequence for preparations might therefore be as follows:

1. Planners will hopefully want to make their decisions about the staging of the implementation process, and about the content and structure of the different stages of training that will be needed to support it, in consultation with appropriate representatives of those whom the process will involve, namely local teachers, teacher educators and institutional leaders. If all these people are to be able to participate in any meaningful manner, they will need to understand what changes are proposed for what purposes and what they imply for classroom teaching and learning. Hence, one of the first things that planners might wish to do is to arrange appropriate awareness-raising meetings with each of the above groups as proposed in sections 9.4.1–9.4.3.

2. Once those directly involved have been introduced to the changes and to their roles in the implementation process, planners will be able to work with representatives of each group to make decisions about what is likely to be the most urgent issue, the content and structure of pre-implementation teacher training. A possible planning sequence would be to:

   (a) decide, bearing local classroom conditions and existing teacher (and teacher educator) strengths in mind, which aspects of the new curriculum should be emphasized when implementation begins
   (b) agree what new understandings and skills it will be essential for teachers to have in order to be able to begin such implementation
   (c) agree how much time can be made available, where training should take place and an approximate set of priorities for what has been agreed at (b)

(d) agree on whether the training should cover all teachers, or just some, and if the latter, which?

(e) assess the extent to which the professional background of the local teacher educators is suitable for helping teachers to develop such skills/ understandings

(f) agree what trainer training might be needed to bridge any obvious gaps

(g) arrange for such trainer training if time, funds and availability of trainer trainers allow

(h) agree dates for the pre-implementation teacher training to take place

(i) try and ensure that sufficient copies of the new materials are available for all teachers and teacher educators well before the training takes place

If it is not possible to provide necessary trainer training then (b) and (c) will need to be reconsidered to make them achievable with the training skills available.

3. To be able to decide about the structure and duration of ongoing training provision, planners, again with representatives of each above group as appropriate, would need to:

(a) agree, given local conditions, which further aspects of the new curriculum it is reasonable to expect all schools to aim to implement within the first year or two of the process

(b) agree what new understandings and skills teachers will need to develop to be able to extend the range of their implementation to cover the above aspects

(c) (bearing funding in mind) agree on the staffing, frequency and structure of such training

(d) (in consultation with institutional leaders) agree procedures for enabling such ongoing training to take place during teachers' working hours

(e) agree a school-based system to monitor the implementation process, identify any widespread problems and communicate these to institutional leaders and local educational administrators/planners

4. Having established the training provision, and through so doing also the extent to which initial implementation of the new curriculum will need to be adjusted to meet local classroom realities, the next area for consideration is awareness raising. For teachers, teacher educators and institutional leaders, this will hopefully have happened at (1) above. The main group not yet drawn into the implementation process is members of the wider community, particularly parents. Decisions about how to communicate with parents with secondary school children will need to be taken.

5. Detailed planning, beyond the establishment of monitoring systems and communication channels that will enable local planners to keep abreast of what is actually happening in their schools, and so be able to use whatever funding they have available for implementation support as effectively as possible, is unlikely to

be possible before implementation begins. To use funding effectively, once implementation is under way local leaders will need to monitor two parallel but interdependent strands of the process. The first is the need to continue to provide appropriate support to bridge the professional and attitudinal gaps among relevant groups of people, principally teachers. The second is to consider local language-teaching conditions and how, over time, these may be made more supportive of both the immediate implementation process and the achievement of its ultimate goals. Other local leaders in contextually similar areas of the country are a potential source of support and also of ideas. Establishing links and regular meetings would be worthwhile.

## 9.6 Conclusion

In sections 9.4 and 9.5 I have tried to show the implications for planning of the main issues arising from Tables 9.3 and 9.4. You will have noticed that I have been able to deal with them only in general terms. This inability to plan in detail much beyond the very beginning of an implementation process is one result of recognizing that complex educational-change implementation as a process depends on the responses of a wide range of people (and often organizations) in a particular setting to whatever reculturing the change implies.

If I say that rational and coherent pre-planning can only take one as far as the early implementation stages, you might be wondering why I have spent so many pages illustrating how to set about gathering information to inform such planning! My response would be that the beginning of a change process is an extremely important indicator of what is (or is not) likely to happen next. If the change process begins with the majority of the people affected feeling that they understand what is happening and why, that they are being supported in their roles and that their immediate educational environment is supportive, they are more likely to be prepared to invest time and energy in developing the new skills (and more complexly, eventually new ways of thinking) that so much educational change demands. If they begin implementation viewing the change as both worthwhile and achievable, they are more likely to invest energy over time in trying to achieve it despite the unanticipated problems that will arise time and again throughout the process. In a context where most of those involved in the change process are positively inclined, I believe that the process is likely to move more directly and more swiftly (although not necessarily *very* directly or swiftly!) towards the hoped-for outcomes than in a context where information about, and support for, the change is patchy or non existent. Time spent on understanding the change context and using that understanding in implementation planning is in my opinion very worthwhile.

Chapter 10

# Planning the development of a new initial teacher education curriculum

In chapters 8 and 9 I looked at how the two sets of questions might guide planning for changes in what happens in college/school classrooms. Here I use the same questions to identify issues relevant to the planning of changes to an initial teacher-education curriculum for English teachers.

## 10.1 Background

A Minister of Education acknowledges that after over a decade of substantial financial and human investment in the teaching of English (for example, the employment of numerous, expensive, expert, national and international consultants to advise on the content and sequence of a new 'communication-based' curriculum, the design and writing of a set of new textbooks and ICT learning materials linked to this curriculum, short training courses for all serving teachers and opportunities for some of them to visit English speaking countries), less than 5 per cent of learners leave secondary school with a basic ability to communicate in English, as measured by a pass in the lowest level of an international standardized test of performance. In addition, the results of a recent test of English teachers' language proficiency were very disappointing.

The focus of all the above planning and investment has (apparently not very successfully) been on the development of a new curriculum and linked materials and trying to enable its implementation by existing teachers in schools. However, there has so far been no change to the pre-service, university-based training of new English teachers. They continue to be trained with little apparent regard for graduating teachers who are well prepared to help learners achieve the hoped-for outcomes of the new school curriculum.

In this country, as seems to be the case in several contexts, the responsibility for providing initial teacher training is divided between staff from two different university departments. Staff from the language departments provide the subject specialist training in language (linguistics, phonetics, grammar and language proficiency work) and culture (the literature and history of English-speaking countries). They also supervise the in-school practical element of the training. The length and format of this varies from one university to the next, but it always ends with an assessed 'exam' lesson. A pass in this is required for qualification as a teacher. The other group of staff from education departments is responsible for generic courses in education (for example, Psychology, History of Education, Evaluation and Assessment, Classroom Management). In most universities there is no professional connection between the two departments, and trainees have long complained that their programme lacks coherence.

The Ministry of Education asks the heads of language departments in the universities that are responsible for providing such initial training to propose a draft outline of, and a detailed rationale for, a new pre-service English-language teacher curriculum that will more clearly link what trainees experience during their studies to the real teaching roles they will be expected to play when they enter the secondary-school system. They set a deadline of one year for this planning process. This chapter considers some of the questions it would be useful for these university curriculum planners to ask and find answers to, to guide their planning of a teacher-training curriculum that better prepares its novice teachers for the classroom conditions in which they will find themselves.

As before I pose and try to answer two sets of questions.

## 10.2 Questions

The first set of questions aims to identify those who will be most directly affected by any changes to the initial teacher-training curriculum and to obtain a sense of their current understandings, skills, beliefs and behaviours.

---

QUESTION TO CONSIDER
- Who might these people be in any initial teacher-training environment?
- What questions would you want to ask (about) them?

---

The second set asks questions about features of the existing conditions in which initial teacher training takes place, and also about aspects of the schools in which trainees will eventually work, and what these imply for the content and process of any new initial teacher-training curriculum.

---

QUESTION TO CONSIDER
- Which of the conditions influencing the existing teacher training and school English-teaching systems would it be relevant to consider?
- What questions would you want to ask about them?

---

## 10.2.1 Questions about who will be affected

As always there are a range of different groups of people who will be more or less directly affected by, and whose behaviours and beliefs will influence the implementation of, any suggested changes to the initial teacher-education curriculum. In this setting these include:

- The university English-specialist teacher educators, whose knowledge and teacher-teaching skills represent the existing subject teacher-training capacity. This may not necessarily be adequate for a new curriculum that tries to prepare teachers to implement the national English curriculum in secondary school classes. Some staff capacity-building may be necessary.
- The university Education-specialist teacher educators who give the same generic courses to all trainee teachers regardless of their subject specialism. At present, the education courses are not linked in any way to the other courses that trainee language teachers follow. Ideally, staff from the Education department would be involved in discussions about how any new curriculum might better highlight the connections between generic and specialist modules.
- Trainees. They come into teacher training bringing with them certain (probably unarticulated) beliefs about (language) learning and teaching drawn from their long experience as school learners. It is necessary to understand what they 'bring with them', so that plans for the new curriculum bear these in mind when deciding on content and teaching approaches.
- Those working with trainees in schools, the supervising teachers or mentors. Ideally they will be involved in the planning process because they will need to be helped to understand what any new curriculum is trying to achieve if they are to support trainees appropriately while they are on school-based teaching practice.
- Secondary-school language learners. What do they expect of their teachers? Are there any general characteristics that need to be considered?

Less directly affected/influential may be:

- Institutional leaders at secondary schools. They will have expectations about the teaching skills, and professional and personal behaviours that novice teachers ought to have.
- Society in general. There will probably be certain unstated expectations of what teachers 'should be like' and how they should behave, deriving from the national educational culture. (Since the possible influence of educational culture was discussed quite thoroughly in the previous scenario, I will not discuss it further here.)

Some questions that local-change leaders could usefully ask about each group are suggested in Table 10.1.

**Table 10.1**  Questions that might be asked of (about) the people most affected by the change.

| Who will be affected | Questions |
|---|---|
| Specialist teacher educators | • What view of teacher learning do they have?<br>• What are their areas of subject strength?<br>• Are both of the above appropriate for what trainees will need to be helped to know, understand and be able to do if they are to implement the school curriculum?<br>• What relationship do they have with members of the education department? |
| Members of the Education department | • What view of teacher learning do they have?<br>• What are their areas of subject strength?<br>• How do they understand the connection between their courses and those offered by subject specialists?<br>• What relationship do they have with members of the Language department? |
| Supervisors/mentors in schools | • What links exist between them and the university subject specialists?<br>• What approaches to language teaching are they most familiar/comfortable with?<br>• How do they understand their role in teacher training process? |
| Language learners | • What roles do they expect teachers to play?<br>• What is their attitude to learning English? |
| School heads | • What understandings, skills and behaviours do they expect from newly graduating teachers? |

## 10.2.2 Questions about the existing conditions in initial English teacher training and school English learning

Conditions that it could be wise to investigate include:

- how training time is currently divided between specialist and Education courses, and whether this is open to negotiation
- the current weightings within specialist courses between different strands of the programme (knowledge about language, developing language proficiency, literature and culture, subject-specific pedagogy/methodology and time spent in schools)
- the assumptions about what teachers need to know about and be able to do that underlie the new school English curriculum and its associated teaching materials
- the systems that currently exist for communicating and working collaboratively with the mentor teachers who support trainees during their school practice
- the number of children in most secondary-school classes and the number of hours of English they have each week

- the resources that trainees can expect to find in most classrooms
- the types and degree of support that novice teachers can expect to receive from the school community when they first arrive

You may think that anyone professionally involved at a senior level in teacher education ought to know the answers to most of these questions already, and so there is little point in asking them. I would agree that some people might, more or less consciously, know the answers to some or even all of them. However, planning a coherent and contextually feasible initial teacher-education curriculum again involves consideration of a range of issues. I therefore feel that even if some planners feel they know 'all the answers', it is still useful to gather all such answers and display them, so that they are available to inform the implementation discussions that will be necessary before any final decisions are made. Some questions, derived from the bullet points above, are shown in Table 10.2.

Table 10.2

| Condition | Questions |
|---|---|
| Division of training time between Education and the specialism | • What proportion of the overall time is taken up by Education/specialist courses?<br>• Is this balance about right?<br>• What would the procedure be for opening discussions about possible changes to the content and/or manner of provision? |
| Weightings in current specialist curriculum | • What proportion of the current curriculum time do specialist courses spend on:<br>  • knowledge about language?<br>  • developing language skills?<br>  • Literature and Culture?<br>  • developing language-teaching skills?<br>  • understanding and becoming familiar with working in real classrooms?<br>• Will these proportions need to be adjusted if the new training programme is to support implementation of the school curriculum? |
| The school curriculum and teaching materials | • What are the expected outcomes of the school English curriculum?<br>• What do teachers need to know and be able to do to be able to help learners to achieve them?<br>• What level and type of support do the teaching materials provide for teachers? |
| Cooperating teachers/ mentors | • How are they chosen?<br>• How does the university communicate with them?<br>• How does the university view their role?<br>• What do they gain from taking on the role?<br>• Will changes to the initial teacher-training curriculum require them to change what they do/how they behave? |

| Class sizes and hours per week | • What is the normal class size for a secondary-school language class?<br>• How many hours of English do they have per week?<br>• Do the above influence how teachers need to work in order to complete the curriculum? |
|---|---|
| Classroom resources | • Will all learners have copies of the new textbooks?<br>• What resources can be found in most classrooms?<br>• Do most schools have computer laboratories/rooms for language study?<br>• What aspects of teaching–learning technology do trainees need to know about and be able to use? |
| Support from school community | • Is there a structured induction into school life for novice teachers?<br>• What aspects of school life would it be useful for them to get to know about and experience during their school practice periods?<br>• What does the above imply for the number/length/content/process of these teaching practice periods? |

## 10.3 Answering the questions

In contrast to chapter 9, here answers to many of the above questions will be found within the teacher-training institution itself, or within the schools to which trainees are normally sent for their periods of teaching practice. Some answers may also be found in documents. They ought therefore to be fairly quickly and easily obtainable. However, universities as organizations often have complex internal relationships. Planners may therefore need to be diplomatic at times, especially when dealing with information relating to the weighting of current curriculum provision, since some staff may see any changes to the status quo as professionally threatening.

**Table 10.3**   Answers to questions about people.

| Questions | Answers |
|---|---|
| **Language specialists**<br>What view of teacher learning do they have? | • This varies greatly, but many staff regard themselves primarily as university lecturers. They see their subjects as largely content-based and teach them mostly through lectures, in what they consider to be an appropriately academic manner. |
| What are their areas of subject strength? | • Linguistics, Applied Linguistics, Phonetics, Grammar, Literature, History, language-skills development and, to a lesser extent, Methodology. |

| | |
|---|---|
| Are both of the above appropriate for what trainees will need to be helped to know, understand and be able to do if they are to implement the new curriculum in schools? | ● Given that the school curriculum that trainees will be expected to teach emphasizes enabling learners' language skills development, in many cases neither some of the teaching approaches used nor the theoretical content seem appropriate. |
| What relationship do they have with members of the education department? | ● Little or no contact. The modules from each department run in parallel. There has never been any formal discussion of whether or how they might be better linked. |
| **Education specialists**<br>What view of teacher learning do they have? | ● They view trainee teachers like any other undergraduates. They teach the mostly factual content of their courses through lectures. |
| What are their areas of subject strength? | ● Educational Psychology, Evaluation and Assessment, the history and current features of the national education system, and other generic courses of potential relevance to all teachers |
| How do they understand the connection between their courses and those offered by subject specialists? | ● Most staff do not appear to consider the specialism of the students that they teach to be relevant. |
| What relationship do they have with members of the Language department? | ● Little or no personal contact and no formal professional contact. |
| **Trainees**<br>What experience of (language) learning do they bring with them from secondary school? | ● A broadly transmission-based approach to learning generally. Memorization very important for exam success. Some will have had occasional experience of more interactive methods from their language classrooms. |
| What level of language proficiency do they arrive with? | ● A very low level of performance. Some know a lot about English. Very few can use what they know. |
| How similar/different are these to the understandings/teaching skills/level of proficiency that they will need to develop to be able to implement a version of the new school curriculum? | ● Different. The curriculum expects learners to leave school able to use the language at a basic level. This suggests that their teachers need to:<br>  ● be confident enough about their own language proficiency to teach mostly in English<br>  ● know enough about how language works to be able to provide learners with a clear grounding in the sound and grammar systems |

| | |
|---|---|
| | • understand enough about how languages are learned, and be confident enough about their teaching skills, to be able to manage both teacher-led and interactive classroom activities that are appropriate for their learners' ages and levels |
| **Cooperating teachers/mentors**<br>What links exist between them and the university subject specialists? | • Such teachers have been appointed by their Heads. They receive necessary paperwork from the university, but have no direct professional links. |
| How do they understand their role in the teacher-training process? | • As supervisors who will (initially) help trainees plan their classes. They are expected to remain in the classroom when trainees are teaching to evaluate their work and to assist with any classroom-management issues. |
| What approaches to language teaching are they most familiar/comfortable with? | • As classroom teachers who have had only a single short period of in-service training they often struggle to teach the new curriculum. Many focus on the more familiar reading and grammar sections of the textbook in great detail, and ignore the sections devoted to the development of other language skills. |
| **Learners**<br>What roles do they expect teachers to play? | • They expect teachers to manage all learning and to highlight what needs to be learned (memorized) through the notes they write on the board. |
| What is their attitude to learning English? | • Many learners see no point in learning the language. It plays no obvious role in their daily lives outside the classroom and is not assessed in any high-stakes examinations. |
| **Institutional heads**<br>What understandings, skills and behaviours do they expect from newly graduating teachers? | • They expect newly appointed teachers to be able to manage classes, teach the curriculum, as well as is possible in the circumstances that exist in the school, and to teach the allocated textbook at the same speed as other teachers in their year.<br>• They expect them to be neat, polite, punctual and willing to work hard. |

Answers to these questions already suggest aspects of the existing training curriculum that need thinking about if trainees are to be better prepared for implementing the school curriculum. The picture becomes even clearer when the next set of questions are answered.

**Table 10.4**   Answers to questions about existing conditions.

| Questions | Answers |
|---|---|
| **Division of training time between the two departments**<br>What proportion of the overall time is taken up by Education/specialist courses? | • There is approximately a 30% Education/70% specialist subject split. |
| Is this balance about right? | • It could be if the two 'sides' of the training became more clearly linked. |
| What would the procedure be for opening discussions about possible changes to the content and/or manner of provision? | • Head of the specialist programme would in the first place need to talk to the head of the Education department, and later to individual staff offering Education modules. |
| **Weightings in specialist curriculum**<br>What proportion of the current curriculum time do specialist courses spend on:<br>  • knowledge about language/ linguistics/grammar, etc.?<br>  • developing personal-language skills?<br>  • Literature and Culture?<br>  • developing language-teaching skills?<br>  • understanding and becoming part of real classrooms/teaching practice? | <br><br><br>20%<br>10%<br>20%<br>5%<br><br>15% |
| Are these proportions appropriate for the new training curriculum? | • No, the balance seems to be too heavily weighted towards the provision of 'knowledge'. The proportion of time spent on the development of personal-language proficiency and the range of teaching skills needed to implement the new school curriculum seems insufficient. |
| **School curriculum and teaching materials**<br>What are the expected outcomes of the school English curriculum? | • Learners who can pass an internationally validated and standardized test of performance at basic level. |
| What do teachers need to know and be able to do to be able to help learners to achieve them? | • Know about language and how to help learners to know about it too and become confident enough to use what they know for simple interactional and transactional purposes. Trainees need to |

| | |
|---|---|
| | feel confident about their personal linguistic proficiency and their teaching abilities to manage a class, use a range of activities, interact with learners, recognize not all learners are the same, adjust, be flexible, etc. |
| ● What level and type of support do the teaching materials provide for teachers? | The set of textbooks that operationalizes the curriculum comes with teachers' books that offer step by step guidance for each lesson, and also provide links to the parallel computer-based materials. |
| **Cooperating teachers/mentors** How are they chosen? | ● According to years of teaching experience. |
| How does the university communicate with them? | ● The university has no direct professional contact with them. |
| How does the university view their role? | ● They should be in class with trainees at all times. They are there to evaluate trainees, ensure they teach for the specified number of hours, help them with preparation/ classroom management as necessary. |
| What do they gain from taking on the role? | ● No tangible benefits, apart from the opportunity to work with trainees (who take most responsibility for teaching their classes for several weeks each year). |
| Will changes to the initial teacher-training curriculum require changes in what is expected of them? | ● Yes. Exactly what changes will depend on how the role of the teaching practise is conceptualized in the new curriculum. |
| **Class sizes and hours per week** What is the normal class size for a secondary-school language class? | ● 45 learners. |
| How many hours of English do they have per week? | ● 3–4. |
| Do the above influence how teachers need to work in order to complete the curriculum? | There is insufficient time to complete the whole textbook. Teachers are implicitly pressured to 'finish' the book by the end of the year, since annual tests are based on the content. This works against teachers using the book flexibly, making principled choices, adapting the materials to their learners' needs, etc. |
| **Classroom resources** Will all learners have copies of the new textbooks? | ● Yes. |
| What technological resources can be found in most classrooms? | ● None. |

| | |
|---|---|
| Do most schools have computer laboratories/rooms for language study? | • Yes. One hour per class per week. Computer room with one computer between two learners and pre-installed software and access to the internet. |
| What aspects of teaching–learning technology do trainees need to know about and be able to use? | • Trainees will need to know something about the type of software that is used in schools and what aspects of language development it is thought to support, how to manage learning in the computer room and what types of materials on the internet can be used to support language learning. |
| **Membership of the school community** Is there a structured induction into school life for novice teachers? | • No. |
| What aspects of school life would it be useful for them to learn about and experience during their school-practice periods? | Some might be: <br> • Teacher–learner relationships. <br> • Relationships between colleagues. <br> • Communication systems in schools – finding things out, whom to go to for what information. <br> • Schools as organizations. How does the hierarchy work, and how are relations managed between leaders and led? <br> • Where extra materials can be found/ where photocopying, etc. is done. <br> • Any particular school rituals. |
| What does the above imply for the number/length/content/process of these teaching-practice periods? | • Teaching practice probably needs to be in several phases. A first phase could perhaps be spent as a 'classroom assistant' to the mentor teacher, enabling trainees both to observe language teaching and learning in the classroom and to develop a sense of 'how things are done' in the wider school environment. Later phases could involve taking some, and eventually complete, responsibility for teaching a class. |

The information in Table 10.4 provides further guidance to curriculum planners. It identifies issues that will need to be addressed if the new curriculum is to enable initial trainees to graduate as novice teachers, able to 'fit' into existing schools and teach in a manner that at least reflects the spirit of what the school English curriculum is trying to achieve.

## 10.4 Using information to inform decision making

There seem to me to be a number of problems with the programme that is currently offered.

> QUESTION TO THINK ABOUT
> From the answers in Tables 10.3 and 10.4, what do you consider the main problems to be?

I see the following as important.

### 10.4.1 The content of the existing specialist curriculum

The emphasis here is very much on giving trainees (more or less) relevant knowledge about language, how language works, and about the history and literature of the cultures in which the language has developed. Relatively little time is spent on ensuring that trainees' own level of language is high enough for them to feel confident about using the language to teach with, and on developing their understanding of the curriculum that they will be expected to teach and the complex ability to flexibly use a range of techniques, activities and materials to do so. In addition there seems to be little thought given to the potential that the training period offers for explicitly discussing trainees' beliefs about (language) learning and how these differ from those underlying the school curriculum, and for modelling of the desired flexible, learner-sensitive teaching by university staff. Finally, the role of the teaching practice within the curriculum will need reconsideration, to try to maximize its value as a linking mechanism between the training programme and the classroom.

### 10.4.2 The content and role of the Education modules

These currently make no attempt to show how an understanding of generic educational issues and/or principles is relevant to subject-specific study. Nor is there any rationale for their positioning within the curriculum. Could they be adjusted to become more relevant to the needs of trainee language teachers? For example, could a generic course in Classroom Management introduce techniques for managing learners working in groups, or provide principles for/practice in giving clear instructions for activities that learners are expected to do without teacher supervision? Could a course in Psychology have a section dealing with affective factors in the classroom, introducing ideas about how 'motivation' is currently understood and what this implies for teaching approaches that might be used to strengthen learners' motivation? What negotiations and preparations would such adjustments to the content, and perhaps the timing, of education modules entail? Who would need to be involved? Would relationships between staff in the two departments need to become more collaborative? How might that be made possible?

## 10.4.3 The relationship between staff at the university and the mentors in practice schools

Under the present model there seems to be minimal contact between the university staff, who have overall responsibility for the training programme, and the mentor teachers in schools who play such a potentially important role in supporting the transition from the study setting to the professional working environment. If the new training curriculum considers teaching practice to be an important strand of the training process, there will need to be better communication with and support for mentor teachers. There will also need to be channels through which they can feed into the content of, and teaching approaches used during, the training programme in the light of their ongoing experiences of trainees' strengths and weaknesses. The traditionally hierarchical relationship in which university teachers consider that they have little or nothing to learn from those working in schools, is quite inappropriate for those training teachers in universities, for whom the school-based mentors ought to represent colleagues who can make potentially invaluable, context-informed contributions to the overall success of the training programme.

The current initial teacher-training programme is provided by at least three disparate 'groups' (within which there are numerous subgroups, for example the Linguists, the Phoneticians, the Grammarians, the Literature teachers, the Methodologists, the Psychologists and the History of Education specialists) who work with little or no reference to, or understanding of, what other groups are doing, or of how what they do contributes to the overall training of the language teacher. Greater coherence between what each group contributes to the 'whole' curriculum is clearly desirable. However, before they can begin to work out the (potential) contribution that each group can make to a new, more coherent, curriculum, planners will need to develop a 'vision' of the sort of trainee that they wish to develop.

> QUESTION TO CONSIDER
> If you were asked to develop such a 'vision', what would you base your 'vision' on?

Some more or less idealistic and/or pragmatic bases around which such a 'vision' might be developed include:

- the idea of a teacher as someone able to implement the new school English curriculum. What are the features of such an English teacher?

- the idea of the teacher as a social-change agent. What are the features of such an (English) teacher?
- the idea of a teacher who 'fits' easily into the national/local educational culture. What are the features of such a teacher?
- a vision based purely on the training resources currently available in the training environment. What type of knowledge and skills can the existing staff realistically provide? What kind of (English) teacher will this lead to?
- a vision based mainly around theories about language, (language) learning, (language) teaching, (language) assessment. What do these theories suggest that a good language teacher knows, is able to do and believes about his own and others' learning?
- a purely pragmatic view based around the secondary-school classroom reality. What does a trainee need to know, understand and be able to do, if s/he is to be able to work effectively with very variably motivated learners in (by my standards) a fairly large class?

Whatever 'vision' is agreed will probably represent a compromise between idealism and pragmatism. Some issues that may influence the nature of the compromise are suggested below.

- The weighting of specialist modules.
  - If this is to be changed, there will be implications for the staff who teach modules that are deemed unnecessary
  - What will their roles be in the new curriculum?
  - Will there be funding for capacity-building?
  - Will they be willing to develop new skills?

- The number and content of education modules.
  - Which are potentially relevant? Which seem less so?
  - How can relevant modules be more clearly linked with the needs of specialist trainees?
  - Can those that seem less relevant be cut from the curriculum?
  - Who would have the final say about the above questions? How could they be approached?

- The certification of trainees' language proficiency.
  - Should trainees have to pass a recognized language exam in order to graduate?
  - Should trainees whose language development is too slow (as measured by some agreed marker) be removed from the programme?
  - When?
  - How much language-development work will be needed to achieve whatever goal is decided on?

- If an underlying principle of the new curriculum is that the teaching trainees receive from university staff during their language development (and other courses) should aim to model the type of teaching we hope they will be doing by the time they graduate:

- What changes does this imply for the way in which language (or other subjects) are taught and assessed?
- Are current staff able to make such changes?
- Ehat capacity-building would be needed over what length of time?
- Is funding likely to be available?

- The subject methodology modules.
  - How many of these modules should there be?
  - What aspects of teaching should they focus on?
  - How closely should they be linked to the teaching-practice periods?

- Teaching-practice periods in schools.
  - How often and when should they take place?
  - How long for?
  - What is/are their role(s)?
  - What support/encouragement/opportunities to participate will the university need to provide for mentor teachers in order to enable them in turn to support trainees appropriately?

- Assessment of trainees' teaching ability/skill.
  - Does being assessed on a single exam lesson 'fit' the principles underpinning whatever 'vision' has been agreed?
  - What and/or who will need to be developed/prepared for an alternative approach to assessment to be implemented?

Reaching a conclusion about the curriculum 'vision' requires juggling a huge range of factors. The decisions that are made will potentially affect a large number of colleagues in both schools and the university. The final section below suggests an order in which the planning process might proceed.

## 10.5 Deciding on an order in which to make the preparations

This book has frequently stressed the desirability of involving as many representatives as possible of those affected by the change in decision making at all stages of the change process. Here I find myself slightly contradicting what I have said earlier, since for the sake of practicality I suggest that only a small group of people should be involved in the first stage of the suggested process below.

1. Given the range of factors that will need to be considered, I see the first stage as involving only the (probably) small group of staff from the specialist department who have been charged with leading the planning process. I assume that if questions similar to those above have been asked, it is they who will probably have asked them, and they who will have spent time thinking about the answers and

what they imply. I therefore think (given that there is a deadline) that it would be most practical for them to develop a first draft of, and rationale for, the 'vision' and its main implications for the curriculum content and process.

2. At the next stage everyone immediately affected needs to be given the opportunity to become involved. One means of enabling this would be to hold a well-publicized open meeting to which members of the three groups responsible for providing training are invited. Ideally, Education staff, school-based mentors and any Language staff likely to find suggested curriculum changes difficult would be invited personally by a senior member of the 'core' planning group at (1). In my experience, an interested minority ('vanguard teachers', see chapter 2.1) will attend. At this meeting the drafts developed at (1) above will be shared with everyone, and those present will have the opportunity to comment/ask questions. The meeting will also provide an opportunity to invite representatives from each interested group to join the planning team.

3. Depending on the nature of comments made/questions asked, the now aug-mented planning team may need to have one or more a further meetings to redraft (1) and one or more further versions of ( 2) to present the new versions, until a widely agreed set of principles underlying the change, and a new weighting of curriculum content that is consistent with the principles, is reached.

4. At this point the planning group may need to split up according to the 'strands' of the curriculum (language, literature and culture, language proficiency, subject pedagogy, education, teaching practice) to consider questions such as those below.

- What each strand (potentially) contributes to the new curriculum.
- What this means in practice in terms of what modules should be trying to achieve.
- What the human-resource implications are.
- What capacity-building work would be needed before and during implementation to enable university-/school-based staff to fulfil their roles.

This process is likely to involve cycles of working as sub-groups and reporting back to the whole group, before the content an sequence of the new curriculum becomes clear enough for a draft curriculum to be drawn up.

5. A meeting similar to that at (2) at which the draft curriculum is presented and explained, and at which comments and questions are solicited. It is only at this stage, when the proposed change takes the tangible form of new draft curriculum, that 'winners' and 'losers' emerge in the form of those whose sub-specialisms have 'won' or 'lost' prominence within the new draft. A period of negotiation, adjustment and compromise is virtually certain to follow, before a final version of a new curriculum (together with a rationale and suggestions for the capacity-

building support that will be needed) can be agreed by most of those who will be involved should it be implemented.

6. This final version can then be presented to the Ministry as a document that is widely (although almost certainly not fully) supported by those whom it affects in the university that has proposed it.

## 10.6 Conclusion

This section of the book has tried to demonstrate a means whereby change-planners might begin to gather information to guide their future action. The tables and bulleted lists give an illusion of neatness, certainty and precision that cannot fully represent the process when real people are trying to plan in real change settings. Nonetheless, I hope you see that through a process that begins by asking fairly simple questions it is possible to obtain a wealth of information that can usefully inform the decision-making process at either the initial planning stage (chapter 10) and/or the planning for implementation stage (chapters 8 and 9). Even where the questions seem simple and the answers self-evident, I believe that consciously going through the process, even if only quickly, remains a worthwhile awareness-raising exercise in itself. It will at the very least make it more difficult for planners to ignore important features of their baseline context when making their implementation plans.

I would like to make a few observations about fundamental aspects of educational change that I feel have been illustrated or reinforced in this section of the book.

1. Although educational-change initiatives can vary greatly in their scale, the questions that planners would be wise to ask to obtain information to inform their implementation planning, and the range of information that answers can provide, are the same for smaller-scale changes (chapters 8 and 10) and larger-scale ones (chapter 9).

2. Where an educational change is introduced nationally, the form in which it is initially implemented will need to vary to accommodate different local human and material resources (chapter 9). This is normal, since no country is completely homogeneous in every way. What I believe matters at the beginning of the implementation stage, is not whether all examples of implementation are identical, but instead whether the majority of local attempts at change implementation are genuinely trying to introduce at least some of the spirit of the change to their classrooms. This is much more likely to be so, if the initiation stage of the change has tried to help all those affected to understand what that spirit is (see Table 4.1 in the Conclusion to section 1). For example, if a central aim of the national change is to introduce learning activities that will promote greater interaction between learners in their classrooms, then any initial implementation attempts that do try to incorporate such activities, even if (due to local variables) only

occasionally and imperfectly to begin with, is in my opinion implementing change. Assuming that appropriate on-going implementation support is available and continues to be provided, greater convergence towards the desired change practices is likely to occur over time as local expertise and confidence develop.

3. The national policy makers in chapter 7 (in section 2) provided only an outline framework to guide the implementation of their change. I suggested that this was appropriate for a national change that will affect very large numbers of learners, since national policy makers, even if they carried out a thorough 'baseline study', would not be able to anticipate and draw up appropriate plans for all the very different implementation contexts for which they are nominally responsible. What national policy makers can, and ideally will, do is ensure that their local representatives are provided with change-planning-implementation funds and that they are fully briefed about the change, so that local leaders *are* equipped to make appropriate local plans (see Table 4.1, in the Conclusion to section 1). However, even at the local level, as chapter 9 shows, the scope for detailed long-term planning is often limited. While it is possible to plan how to prepare for, begin, and monitor the local implementation of a national change, and to establish systems for supporting teachers once it has begun, it is not possible to plan in detail very far in advance. It is only once implementation is under way that it will become possible to see exactly what aspects of change implementation are most problematic and so plan to provide appropriate further support.

This idea that even at local level, detailed planning can reach little further than the start of the implementation stage, and that further planning will need to follow based on implementers' lived experience, again highlights the inappropriacy and unhelpfulness of viewing educational-change implementation as a purely rational linear process, whose stages which can be planned in detail, in advance, in a top-down manner.

4. The above points reinforce the importance of recognizing change implementation as a process that evolves (in different ways in different local contexts) rather than as an event that occurs (see chapter 1). They also support the view (raised in chapter 5) that the implementation stage of the process is bound to be cyclical and incremental rather than linear. By this I mean that implementation of educational change can be visualized as an ongoing series of trying out/implementing-monitoring-adapting-trying out/re-implementing-monitoring-adapting . . . cycles. If appropriately supported, the experience of numerous cycles over time will hopefully move implementers closer both to a fuller understanding of the principles underlying the change, and to implementing the fullest version of the change that is compatible with the existing variables in their own evolving context.

# Chapter 11

# Setting the scene for successful change: Beginning at the beginning

In this final short chapter I note a small number of fundamental issues that will need to be addressed before any of the suggestions made in this book can begin to be achieved.

The cases in section 2 and the scenarios in section 3 draw on real-life experiences of educational-change initiatives on four different continents. There are of course geographical, political, socio-economic and cultural differences between and within the various contexts, which also affect their education systems. Despite such differences, I feel that the systems share certain basic features, which make it difficult for them to successfully implement large-scale educational changes that entail any significant degree of reculturing. I believe that these features are also shared, to differing degrees, by state-education systems almost everywhere, and that they help to explain some reasons why the following continues to be true.

> We can produce many examples of how educational practices could look different, but we can produce few, if any, examples of large numbers of teachers engaging in these practices in large-scale institutions designed to deliver education to most children (Elmore 1995 in Fullan 2001: 5).

---

A LAST QUESTION
Can you think of any reasons why there are so few obvious examples of large-scale educational changes that have unambiguously achieved their stated aims?

---

I think some central reasons include the following.

## National educational policy makers are reluctant to acknowledge that many change initiatives start from some version of a 'transmission-based' view of education

I believe that the process of implementing a reculturing of an education system towards a more flexible and dynamic view of teaching and learning continues to represent a considerable challenge for those involved in trying to introduce educational changes in all contexts due to a reluctance to acknowledge where change is starting from.

Over the past decades there has been an enormous volume of public discussion (and academic research) about, for example, the challenges that globalization poses for education, the need to recognize learning as a lifelong process and the roles that technology can play in developing pedagogies that will lead to more interactive and personalized learning opportunities. Despite this discussion, I believe that the longstanding view that the central role of the teacher is to pass on a largely predetermined body of knowledge/set of skills to learners remains deeply embedded within classrooms in many education systems.

What evidence do I have for this claim, other than my own ongoing engagement with education systems in different parts of the world? Since educational cultures are not transparent, it is difficult to collect definitive data about their nature. Support for my assertion comes from an overview of approaches to the teaching and learning (of English) in East Asia (Nunan 2003) and to education more generally in the Organisation for Economic Cooperation and Development (OECD) countries (Riley 2000).

> The prevailing notion of teaching and learning remains one in which, according to an OECD study, knowledge, competencies and values are predefined and stored in curricula, tests and accredited textbooks. (Posch 1996 in Riley 2000: 42)

At the time that the above data was reported on, most OECD members were 'high income' countries from Europe or North America. If this view of teaching and learning prevailed in these countries, despite educational rhetoric espousing very different teaching–learning approaches, then I believe it was likely to be prevalent elsewhere also. OECD is expanding all the time, and its membership is increasingly representatively distributed worldwide. Currently it is carrying out a Teaching and Learning International Survey (TALIS) across member countries. The website suggests that TALIS will provide an overview of teaching practices and beliefs in OECD countries:

> The quality of the learning environment at the classroom level is influenced by the teaching methods and classroom practices used by teachers. TALIS will not measure the effectiveness of teachers or of different teaching practices. Rather, it will contrast profiles of teaching practices, attitudes and beliefs among the participating countries. In terms of teaching practices, survey responses from teachers in TALIS will be summarised to examine whether different teaching practices can be identified, such as practices that

tend to focus on direction from the teacher and others that are more open-ended in their approach. (OECD website, 2008)

TALIS will report in 2009, and the conclusions will provide further evidence as to whether the claim that I make here is valid.

If the claim is true, then in the very competitive twenty-first-century world environment it is not surprising that national-change initiators in most contexts are reluctant to admit (to themselves and the wider world) that some form of a 'transmission based' approach remains the starting point from which many of their teachers, learners, institutional leaders, educational administrators and members of the wider society will begin any personal process of educational change. However, this unwillingness to acknowledge their change participants' starting point, and so to begin their change initiatives 'where people are', makes it impossible for change planning to be situated in the lived reality of those whom the change will affect. Such 'wishful planning' in my opinion contributes greatly to the lack of success characteristic of so many educational change initiatives.

## Little encouragement for people to share personal meanings of key educational concepts

Perhaps because the above view of education is so deeply embedded, there is surprisingly little opportunity and/or encouragement in most education systems that I have encountered (and educational-change processes within them) for teachers, teacher trainers, institutional heads and educational policy makers at all levels to articulate and question what is meant by fundamental educational terms like *teaching–learning–knowing*. Since there is no tradition of discussion, educational changes are often introduced with little examination of the extent to which the achievement of key change aims (for example, *learner-centred-classrooms*) will require people affected by the change to develop a different understanding of these apparently familiar terms. This again represents a lack of consideration of what degree and type of reculturing the rhetoric of change actually entails for those affected, and is, I believe, a further reason for the lack of actual change brought about by many change initiatives.

## Reculturing needs to begin 'above' the teachers

Linked to both of the above, and also to the idea of how people feel about change (see chapter 1.3), is the reality that teachers whose prior experience has been in a broadly transmission-based system will need to feel reasonably confident before they can be expected to be enthusiastic about trying out what for them may be radically new teaching approaches involving unfamiliar ways of configuring and/or managing classes and/or organizing activities that may have multiple possible outcomes. Enabling such confidence is of course the responsibility of those leading the change process. However, if transmission-based views of education remain as deeply embedded, and opportunities to discuss the principles underlying education as few, as I suggest above, then who within the educational setting will have the understandings and skills to be able to help teachers develop such confidence? As Table 4.1 (in the Conclusion to section 1) tries to show, educational changes that require the reculturing of teachers cannot be introduced with any expectation of widespread success, without first beginning to address the necessary reculturing of those whose role it is to support teachers' reculturing.

## Poor communications between the interdependent 'parts' of any education system affect the outcomes of the 'whole'

The cases in section 2 (and also the original examples from which I created the scenarios) suggest that there are frequently poorly developed communication/consultation mechanisms between different levels of education systems, and even between those working at the same level or within the same institution. This may be because broadly transmission-oriented educational cultures tend to be associated with fairly conservative hierarchical organizational cultures (see Figure 3.2) where the development of 'open' channels of communication has not traditionally been a priority.

Within an educational-change process, lack of open communication makes it difficult for change participants working at different levels of, or with different responsibilities for, an educational-change process to see themselves as part of a 'whole' system. They are less likely to be aware of how their 'part' in the change process can contribute positively to the 'whole'. Instead each 'part', if actively participating at all, focuses only on its own contribution. Given that successful implementation, especially of a large-scale educational-change, clearly requires a high degree of collaboration and open and regular communication between large numbers of people, this tendency again seems unhelpful for the successful implementation of educational change.

If educational change is to succeed in any setting, it needs to start from where people are. If the 'gap' between what affected groups of people currently understand and what the change requires them to understand is great, then the necessary preparation for the change will need to take longer. Ultimately, short cuts do not work and introducing change initiatives that ignore this simple truth amounts, in my opinion, to little more than the *symbolic triumphalist action* (Goodson 2001) referred to in section 1.

So at its simplest the message of this book is that if you are actively involved in leading or supporting some or all aspects of an educational change, begin at the beginning with an honest appraisal of the existing realities of the people whom you are responsible for. Once again it is a matter of asking questions and acting on the answers in a way that will support the change process. A basic set of questions for most occasions might be:

1. What ideas about learning and teaching underlie the change? What do these ideas assume people understand and are able to do? What teaching–learning conditions do they assume?
2. To what extent do the people you are responsible for understand what is needed? To what extent can they do what is needed? Are learning conditions adequate to begin implementation?
3. What are the main professional and material gaps between (1) and (2)?
4. What possibilities exist for helping people 'bridge the gaps'? Which of these possibilities can be carried out with existing material and human resources? Can anything be done about material gaps?
5. What opportunities can be offered to 'bridge the gaps' before implementation begins? Once implementation has begun?
6. What is the best way of monitoring what happens in classrooms once implementation begins?
7. In the existing circumstances, what is the best way of continuing to be supportive of the people (or of providing better material conditions) over time?

Participating in an educational-change process in any capacity can be very worrying and tiring. It can also be professionally and personally exciting and rewarding (Oplatka 2005). How you and other people experience the process will very much depend on how well it is managed and led. This book, like any other, cannot possibly anticipate all the factors that might influence how people feel in and react to a particular change process. However, if I am trying to imagine how others might feel or react when confronted with a challenging change, I have always found it helpful to think about how I feel and react when I feel unconfident, and use that as a starting point for any planning that I need to do.

I very much hope that if you are involved in leading or managing educational change in some capacity, you will find that some of the ideas I have suggested make sense and are helpful, and so contribute to making your involvement in the process a more positive experience, both in terms of its effect on you personally and in terms of how what you do affects others. Good luck.

I would be really interested to hear from you, whether about your opinion of this book, or about your educational-change experiences.

My email address is: m.wedell@education.leeds.ac.uk.

Please get in touch.

## References

Elmore, P. (1995), 'Getting to scale with good educational practice', *Harvard Educational Review*, 66/1, 1–26.

Graddol, D. (2006), *English Next*. London: British Council.

Ministry of Education, Culture, Sports, Science and Technology (Japan), 'Regarding the establishment of an action plan to cultivate Japanese with English abilities', www.mext.go.jp/english/topics/03072801.htm (accessed 30 August 2008).

Nunan, D. (2003), 'The impact of English as a global language on educational policies and practices in the Asia-Pacific region', *TESOL Quarterly*, 37/4, 589–613.

OECD, 'Teaching and learning international survey', http://www.oecd.org/document/0/0,3343,en_2649_39263231_38052160_1_1_1_1,00.html (accessed 2 September 2008).

Riley, K. (2000), 'Leadership, learning and systemic reform', *Journal of Educational Change*, 1, 39–55.

Wedell, M. (2003), 'Giving TESOL change a chance: supporting key players in the curriculum change process', *System*, 31/4, 439–56.

# Index